MW00986306

THE ASCENSION PROCESS

Gail Ries

with

Marc Ries

The Other Kingdoms
PO Box 1339
Merlin OR 97532

First Commercial Printing January 2010

Book Creation by M. Ries
Base Space Image Courtesy of NASA

Interior symbols based on
the "MU" books by James Churchwood

ISBN 978-0-615-34085-2 (pbk.)

Printed in America
10 9 8 7 6 5 4 3 2 1

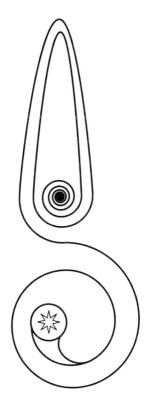

A

STAR CENTER FOR ASCENSION

Publication

TABLE OF CONTENTS

Om Haran Haraya Namaha[*]

(*A Mantra for general well-being*)

Om Eim Hrim Klim Chamundayei Vicche Namaha

(Protection from negative energies)

Om Gum Ganapataye Namaha

(Remove obstacles in one's Path)

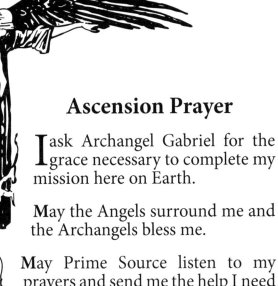

Ascension Prayer

I ask Archangel Gabriel for the grace necessary to complete my mission here on Earth.

May the Angels surround me and the Archangels bless me.

May Prime Source listen to my prayers and send me the help I need to complete my Divine Contract.

May my Ascension be accomplished before the Earth's Ascension and may I be able to see the Earth in all her glory. *Amen.*

—Archangel Gabriel

Dedication

We live on a wonderful jewel of a planet. Whether known as Mother Earth, Gaia, our beloved Vergo, or other names, she is a loving Soul who is a sentient being longing for evolution, growth and yes, Ascension.

God has heard the prayers of Mother Earth and has decided that this time, as she passes over the Galactic Center of our Universe, she will ascend (see "Abraham the Celestial" on page 42). The planets in our solar system are also sentient and will be positively affected by her Ascension Process.

This book is dedicated to Mother Earth and all the Kingdoms who make their home here.

⁓

Quan Yin ⁓ I will tell you that God, in his generosity, is allowing humanity to ascend to the fifth dimension and skip over the fourth [dimension]. This is a great gift and one that benefits humanity because such a jump can often take hundreds of years [or more] in other situations. ✳

"WE WANT TO TELL YOU THAT GOD'S PLAN HAS BEEN CHANGED SEVERAL TIMES. HE ORIGINALLY HAD THE EARTH CHANGES HAPPENING MUCH SOONER. THE ADDITIONAL TIME WAS GIVEN SO MORE COULD AWAKEN AND INDEED, THEY HAVE. HE ALSO HAS CAREFULLY PLANNED MANY OTHER EVENTS TO HELP EVEN MORE AWAKEN." —THE ASCENDED MASTERS

Purification Prayer

I pray for the Violet Flame of Transmutation and Healing to consume my body and all my etheric bodies.

May this violet flame burn away all negativity and disbelief until I shine like the diamond of God's heart.

Amen.

—Saint Germain

Forward

Getting humanity to "Awaken" is like trying to get a tired person out of their bed in the morning; no one wants someone jumping up and down on their bed yelling, "Wake up! It's time to wake up!"

No one likes to be forced to "wake up." Would *you* respond with a "please, get off my bed" or with a "get the <bleep> out of here!"?

God has been trying for centuries to get humanity to Awaken on their own and at their own speed. That time is just about over. If you don't Awaken soon, you will miss the greatest opportunity of this lifetime.

⤳

We can honestly say we do not have all the answers or know how everything works and this is especially true once you cross over from the 3rd dimension into the 4th and higher dimensions.

Even for humans on a spiritual path, the phrase "I do not think you are ready to know" or "your third-dimensional mind would not comprehend" can grow frustrating after a while. Yet it is obvious to us that our personal Guides and Guardians have a tendency to give out only the information that is necessary and relevant for our current level of understanding. Each time we learn from additional lessons appropriate for our Path, we seem to be rewarded with a bit more information. "Divine Timing" appears to be the appropriate keyword.

It is also obvious that there is certain information—like the time of First Contact and when and where certain political, economic, social and Earth changing events will occur—is closely guarded so as to not give those "of the Dark" any advantage and to avoid infringing upon any person's Soul Contract. ✳

The Authors

Gail

In essence, the Ascended Masters have commissioned this book to clarify the Ascension Process because the questions and misconceptions about Ascension are numerous. Their words could have come from the late author Aurelia Louise Jones, who was known for her work in bringing Telos and the messages of the Ascended Masters to the attention of people throughout the world— or from any other person who channels. However, it is not the one doing the channeling that is important but rather that the messages be validated using discernment.

Many will read the words of this book and become stuck on one or two points—others may not believe it at all and that's their choice. The Ascended Masters realize that not everyone is ready to hear their message, but in some a curiosity to learn more may be awakened. To those people I say: read more, learn more (there is a list of suggested reading at the back of this book that might interest the reader).

The point is that Ascension does not happen automatically. You must ask for the *Rites of Initiation*. You must be taught by the Ascended Masters. You must remove all karma from this and past lives. You must be willing to make changes in your habits, your attitude and your ability to love. Love is the fastest way to raise your vibration.

The point that some may find hard to accept is that Ascension is not a process that you experience once. Raising your vibration, growing spiritually and Becoming are things that continue eternally. In the following pages the Ascended Masters give us a glimpse into the higher realms and also discuss why we would want to go there. They also explain why some souls are not ready to ascend and what they can expect as well.

The Ascended Masters of Telos were given this task because of their love and devotion to Mother Earth as well as humanity.

Some will find these messages hard to believe because they go against conventional teachings of our world. That doesn't make them any less truthful. Words will ring as Truth when the reader is in alignment with their higher-self. Essentially this means if you are working toward spiritual growth and you are on your Path, you will find tools like this book to help you and validate your way.

Everyone is given the opportunity to Ascend. This means all walks of life, all races, all ages, and all Kingdoms; no one is excluded. Nor is the opportunity limited to just this lifetime— not everyone will ascend before the Earth's Ascension. But we do not have to worry about those Souls—their Path may be longer but their chance for Ascension will not be denied.

I do suggest that you read this book through first before passing judgment on it. In fact, I recommend reading it more than once. With each reading you will find messages you missed because your understanding will have grown. As you advance spiritually the place on your Path will also change.

Time is growing short. Know that you are loved and supported by Prime Creator ("God"), the Ascended Masters, and all the Kingdoms "of the Light" including the Angelic Kingdom. Blessings.✳

Marc

There was a time, not too long ago, when I thought to myself *is this all there is to my life? Do I want to continue?* I don't remember getting an answer at the time, but looking back, it was probably due to the fact that I was not *listening*. I do believe that moment of personal inquiry was the start of a journey that has lead to my own Awakening. It also led to my being in Mount Shasta, California, in the Summer of 2008.

At Mount Shasta, Gail and I were first introduced to the teachings of Telos and participated in our first *Ascension Ceremony,* one of the last presided over by Aurelia L. Jones. It was not too much longer after that Ceremony that I was able to hear my Guides, as well as to some extent hear, smell, see and/or intuit the presence of other dimensional beings (which I use to help validate and discern the information that Gail channels). The next year during a similar event, we (and around 16 or so other people) witnessed some remarkable orb and UFO phenomena during a night-time visit to the base of Mount Shasta.

Speaking of Mount Shasta and Telos, I would like to say that we have gone out of our way (and so did the Ascended Masters) **not** to include information—*important information*—that Aurelia Jones already covered in her many Telos books (refer to the "Resources and References" on page 119). In a perfect world, one would read her books before reading this book.

I recommend that anyone who feels drawn to the idea of Ascension also look into having your own *Ascension Ceremony* on a monthly basis. More information on how (and why you would want) to do this is in Aurelia's book, *The Ascension Flame of Purification and Immortality*.

Also on a daily basis I use the materials contained in Aurelia's book, *Prayers to the Seven Sacred Flames*. Prayers, affirmations and mantras are indeed tools you can use to raise your frequency—and raising your frequency (vibration/Light) is the best way to meet the Ascension Process head-on.

Finally, I would like to suggest that anyone who has not yet considered or done so, to think about getting a Reiki (or equivalent) Level One (or higher) Attunement. The healing of one's self and others is always a great gift and opportunity. Low cost Reiki Level One (hands-on) classes are being offered in many areas and I know of at least two individuals that have offered free remote attunements for those that could not find, or afford, a local Reiki source.

Both Gail and I now have Reiki Level 3 Attunements. ✳

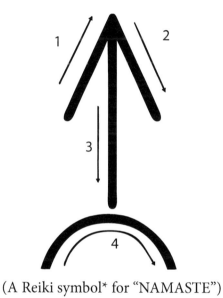

(A Reiki symbol* for "NAMASTE")

....
*   A gift from Archangel Raphael.

Beings of Light

Adama: The High Priest of Telos.

Anahamar: The Twin Flame of Aurelia.

Hilarion: The Keeper of the Temple of Truth.

Lord Lanto: Maha-chohan of the Temple of Wisdom.

Lord Maitraya: The Keeper of the Temple of Resurrection.

Lord Millian: The Keeper of the Temple of Immortality.

Lady Nada: The Twin Flame of Lord Sananda.

Lord Sananda: Known to many as "Jesus" or "Yeshua."

Mother Mary: The mother of "Jesus."

Paul the Venetian: The Keeper of the Temple of Cosmic Love.

Quan Yin: The Goddess of Compassion.

Saint Germain: Ascended Master.

Serapis Bey: The Keeper of the Temple of Ascension.

Shelana: Ascended Master and Spirit Guide.

Basic Definitions

Ascension: The process by which a person/planet leaves their present dimension and goes to a higher one.

Archangels: Creations of God to serve his/her Light.

Ascended Earth: Our current Mother Earth in her fifth dimensional, Ascended form in the Vega Galaxy. See also *Earth1*.

Ascended Master: A spiritually enlightened mortal, not necessarily human, who has undergone the process of Ascension, remains attentive to the spiritual needs of all Kingdoms and acts to inspire and motivate their spiritual growth. They are known as great teachers, healers and Guides and come from all cultures, "religions" and races.

Ascended Masters of Telos: Descendents of Lemuria who are in the fifth (or higher) dimension and now reside in Telos. Some teach in the Ascension temples, some act as Spirit Guides or mentors and some are Keepers of the Temples.

Aura: A field of subtle, luminous energy surrounding a person or object.

Awakening (human): Starting to comprehend the Duality of one's present life, beginning to understand that all things are part of the One and knowing that there is much more to learn spiritually than one has been taught.

Celestials: Creations of God, under the direction of the Archangels, who look after universes and planets under their care.

Chakras: Rotating vortices of life-force energy within the etheric body. The seven basic are the Root, Sacral, Navel, Heart, Throat, Brow and Crown chakras.

Cherubs: Angels who because of their lack of Angelic experience are not quite ready to be full Angels.

Demigods: A creation of God and are under the direction of the Archangels. God gave them the power to create worlds.

Divine Blueprint: The plan which God has for your Soul (the outline of your Soul's purpose).

Divine (Soul) Contract: The agreement you made with your Higher-Self and God before you reincarnated.

Duality: The belief in the idea of separation (good versus bad, male vs female, us vs them, etc.). Thinking of yourself as separated from your Higher Self, and as a result, believing you suffer from lack, and are cut off from God.

Earth1: Our current Mother Earth in her fifth dimensional, Ascended form in the Vega Galaxy. See also *Ascended Earth*.

Earth2: A new Earth-like planet in the Vega Galaxy created for those humans who will ascend before Mother Earth ascends.

Elohim: Angels that look after planetary concerns and are under the direction of the Archangels.

Federation of Light: Fleet of spaceships under the Command of the Federation of Planets, an organization of Enlightened worlds whose purpose is to foster Enlightenment, Brotherhood and Fellowship among the Star races.

Federation of Planets: Organization of Enlightened worlds whose purpose is to foster Enlightenment, Brotherhood and Fellowship among the Star races.

God: The supreme Creator of all-that-is. Also known as Prime Source (typically by those in the Angelic Kingdom) or Prime Creator (typically by the Other Kingdoms).

Greys (Grays): Ancient alien race that has been dieing out for centuries and—in an effort to maintain their numbers—started cloning themselves. Well known for their "abductions" and experiments with DNA and humans.

Higher-Self: The part of your Soul that stays behind when you incarnate. Its purpose is to direct the person on their Divine Path and it gets reunited with your Soul when you die or ascend.

I AM Presence: The original God-spark within us all.

Lightworkers: People who help hold the vibration of Love and Light on the Earth.

Mantra: A sound, word, or phrase that is repeated in prayer— typically 108 times per day for 40 days—and is believed to have mystical powers.

Namaste: An ancient Hindu word with many meanings, including "That which is of God in me greets that which is of God in you."

Of the Dark: One who does not believe they can be forgiven by Prime Creator for past actions, and do not rejoice in God's love.

Reiki: A method of healing, used by the Lemurians according to Ascended Master Sheylana, and reintroduced in modern times by Usui Mikao in 1922. There are three levels of attunement (mastery) including Level 1 (hands-on healing), Level 2 (remote healing) and Level 3 (Master/Teacher). Only Masters can give attunements.

Sacred Initiation Sites: The fifth-dimensional Temples (or Halls) around Earth that represent the Seven Sacred Flames (Ascension, Cosmic Love, Illumination, Resurrection, Truth, Transmutation and the Will of God). Not all of the Temples are located in Telos, some of the Temples do (did) have third-dimensional counterparts and there are more than seven Temples. These sacred sites also correspond to specific chakras, colors, stones, Archangels and Elohim.

Soul Family: Group of souls that were created together, who travel together and have incarnations together.

Soul Group: Souls that come together for a specific purpose or task.

Soul Self: A part of your Soul whose purpose is to be a power of Light to help the person on their Path. It does not get reabsorbed but ceases to exist when the person dies or ascends.

Spirit Guide: Entity who helps a Soul along their spiritual Path and who is in a higher dimension.

Telos: Fifth dimensional city beneath Mount Shasta in California that will be (has been) relocated to Earth2.

Twin Flame: One Soul split apart into male and female energies. Associated with the Darkening of Atlantis.

Veil: Clouds the memory of your past lives, your *Oneness* with the Universe and your real self as a Divine Being. Is something that happens from the time you accept your being born (as you are born) in this lifetime. ✴

Prayer for Awakening

H eavenly Father

I ask for your Light and Love to shine

On those who have not yet Awakened and

Give them the help they need

To see their Path. *Amen.*

—Adama, High Priest of Telos

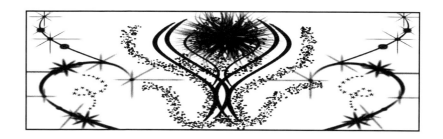

CHAPTER ONE

Greetings!

Greetings! *I am Anahamar* and I welcome you. We will talk about the Ascension Process in more detail than ever before. Our beloved Aurelia* is here with us. Know that she is well and cared for. She did not ascend but that was her choice. She will reincarnate on Earth2 and continue to grow and evolve there.

Greetings! I am Adama and I send you all the love of Telos and the Ascended Masters. We have a special request for you all at this time: we wish you to pray for your fellow humans. It is most important that you understand how the Ascension Process is going. We see so many new students each night and we are gladdened by their enthusiasm. We wish for more of you to come to us for instruction. *Please pray for those yet to Awaken* and know that the time is growing short—you need to Awaken soon if you wish to ascend in this lifetime.

Greetings! I am Aurelia. I am very happy to continue my work from this side and know how much all your love and concern has touched my heart. I will be teaching in the Temple of Immortality where many come to learn about life after "life". It is not mentioned in my Telos books because it was not made known to me at the time. I was not ready for the information.

---

*   Aurelia Louis Jones, author of the *Telos* book series.

We will begin by talking about Ascension. You know through my books that you must receive instruction from the Ascended Masters. Adama says that I am not an Ascended Master, but you may think of me as a teacher. We want to help you through the process. Only when you have cleared your past karmic debt and given your will over to God can you truly be ready for the Ascension Process.

Greetings! I am Sheylana. I am an Ascended Master. I am also a Guide for my beloved Gail. I wish to tell you that she is our very special gift to you. Her role is to light the way and give many of you the tools you will need to ascend. We of Telos love her and thank her for the opportunity to speak our words.

Greetings! I am Lord Sananda. I will tell you why the Ascension Process is so important. Never before has the human race been given this opportunity. You can not only break your cycles of reincarnation, but you can ascend to a higher realm and take your body with you. It will have a physical feel to it, but it will not be as dense. What this means is that the space between your molecules will be wider and they will vibrate at a much higher vibrational level. You will also hold more light as your cells will be more crystalline in nature. This process has begun for many of you who are on the Path of Enlightenment.

Greetings! I am Lord Serapis Bey. I am glad to have this opportunity to speak to you today. We of Telos are so proud of you all. As Lightworkers your light grows stronger and you are coming together in groups for the purposes of spreading love and growing spiritually. Know that I am here to be your teacher and will help all who ask. The Process of Ascension is going to be explained as never before. We want as many as possible to have this information.

Greetings! I am Lord Hilarion. I am so very happy to speak with you. My purpose is to share all the love of the cosmos with you and I expect you to do the same. Go forth and shine your love on everyone you meet. Let the world see your light radiating from your smile and your eyes.

Greetings! I am Lord Lanto. I come with a gift for you. I wish to give you wisdom and illuminate the process you know as Ascension.

Greetings! I am Master Saint Germain. I come to tell you how proud I am of you all. Many of you are seeing my purple light. Know that this is my way of telling you I approve of what you are doing.

Greetings! I am Paul the Venetian. I am here to tell you that my work with you will involve teaching about the principles of healing and transmutation. We will learn how this relates to the Ascension Process.

Greetings! I am Lord Millian. I am not in the Telos books. I will speak to you on learning to incorporate the Light into your meditations.

Greetings! I am Lady Nada. I am the Twin Flame of Lord Sananda. I wish to speak about how you are to live your lives in a world that does not recognize love.

Greetings! I am Lady Quan Yin. I will speak to you about compassion. I will show you how to live your lives open to love and letting your heart lead and not your mind.

Greetings! I am Mother Mary. I am the mother of Lord Sananda. I will speak to you of a mother's love for her child.

Anahamar - You have Aurelia's wonderful books[†] to guide you, but now we will go into even more detail. ∗

[†]   Refer to the "Resources and References" Section.

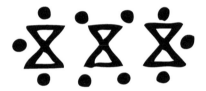

CHAPTER TWO

How It All Started

God Made Many Kingdoms

Archangels and Elohim were created to be part of Prime Creator and do his work. Demigods were created and given the responsibility to create their own universes to control and experiment with. Archangels and Elohim can also create universes, as expressed in Archangel Michael's new "Golden Universe" (*Herst the Dragon* believes it is called 'Golden' because all the planets were made with love and are so beautiful). Celestial Beings were created to look after the universes and planets in their care.

Other Kingdoms came into being when Prime Creator realized that he needed many types of beings to populate these new universes. Prime Creator made Dragons and Fairy People before he had the idea to create "Man".

⌒

Archangel Gabriel ⌒ Celestials are protectors and will do all they can to protect the planets they love.

Pleiadian Collective ⌒ In the beginning [God] made many Kingdoms. He gave his Angels the authority... to create worlds. And so they did. Our race was among the many [God's Angels first] created.[1]

The Planet Mu/Lyra

Lemurian Crystal ⌒ Lemurians used crystals as part of their computer systems. We [the Lemurian Crystals] were once part of a vast computer network.

We of Lemuria came from a planet we called Mu*. The population [there] was very special because they loved God and were of such a vibration that they could feel God's Love. The population of Mu at its greatest was not just in humans, but also Star Brothers and Sisters. The Lemurian people are decedents of the Star race Pleiadians [among others].

Archangel Gabriel ⌒ Mu is/was a very old planet but it was not populated by people on it at first. The Star Brothers and Sisters came to Mu and left some of their people there to inhabit Mu, mostly Arcturians and some Sirians [and Pleiadians].

Mu was also known as Lyra†.

Time passed and the people of Mu evolved and no longer thought of themselves as from the Stars, but rather as people of Mu. They were very loving and very close to God; it was the planet [Mu] that started it all.

Lemurian Crystal ⌒ The Lemurians had no leader because none was needed—they were so highly evolved that they understood that hurting one hurts the all. There was mention of a Ra Mu, but it was not a person. Ra Mu was the spirit of the Mu planet itself, this being a sentient planet like Earth.

Once [upon a time] a planet was aware. It loved the beings that dwelled on its surface. It longed to be more than just a planet

---

*   If you are a follower of Benu's channelings on Mu[2], then Lyra was the original planet and Mu was the first large Earth island the Lemurians inhabited.

†   The Earth, for example, has also been called Gaia, Gula, Beloved Virgo, etc.

because it felt God's Love and wanted to evolve. I can tell you that Mu made a mistake. It asked for help from the Star Brothers and Sisters. They told the planet they could help it evolve by letting it release its very self up to God's Love.

I can say that the planet was told to be very careful how it released its being, but that it wanted so badly to Become, that it did not listen to the people of Mu, but instead let the Star Brothers and Sisters place a device on its surface that would give off enormous amounts of energy—enough to transform the planet. The Device placed on the planet [Mu] did indeed cause the planet to break apart. Do not feel sad for Mu because it did indeed evolve into many nebulas and stars [and a planet]. Mu is very happy and is a very special being.

The Star Brothers and Sisters told the people they would be able to leave Mu and go to a new planet called Earth. The people of Mu learned what was to happen and used their technology to build [star] ships. They left the planet [Mu] and traveled to Earth. All of Mu did not escape—the ships could only hold so many people.

Book of the Dead

Lemurian Crystal ⌒ I have many stories, but this one is not a good one. The people of Mu knew that not everyone would be able to make it off the planet alive. They wished to take as many as possible but this still left a significant number who would perish. This was unacceptable, so the people of Mu asked for help from the Demigods. They told the people of Mu that those who could not fit on the [Star] ship must leave their bodies behind and travel in spirit only. [According to Archangel Gabriel, the Demigods were "not aware" of the Soul Contracts that linked the people of Mu to their planet of birth.]

It was decided that to make this happen, a ritual was evolved whereby the person who was to leave their body would lie down and be anointed with oils and herbs. Then they would slow down their breathing until their heart stopped. Once that happened, their spirit [Soul] would arise from the body and join the group on the ship. Because once on Earth they had no bodies, they were not able to interact and became like ghosts.

Archangel Gabriel ⌒ The Soul, once it leaves the body, is not able to reincarnate unless it goes to the *Temple of Immortality*. The Temple of Immortality has always existed in the 5th dimension for Souls who have been reincarnating on planets. The Temple exists, not on Earth, but in a 5th dimensional realm.

Today it still exists in the same place. The Lost Souls of Mu were not able to go to the Temple because they left their planet of origin [which no longer existed: their "Soul Contracts" were for the original Mu planet]. Similarly, the people of Earth cannot leave Earth and die without losing their chance for their Souls to reincarnate. When the Earth ascends, these Lost Souls of Mu will be forever doomed; they will have no chance for reincarnation nor will they have a place to stay.

God has not decided what to do about them [the Lost Souls of Lemuria]. Praying to God on their behalf is always a good thing.

> **"The Merpeople are Lemurians who decided to live underwater due to the negativity on land."**
> —*ARCHANGEL GABRIEL*

The Lemurians who fled the destruction of their homeland went far and wide; many ended up living in Egypt. The Merpeople are Lemurians who decided [then] to live underwater due to the negativity on land. These Lemurians also called their home planet Mu.

Lemurian Crystal ⌒ The Egyptian "Book of the Dead" is not a memorial to those who died on Mu [but] a bible of how to keep from leaving your body. *The Book of the Dead* is dedicated to these Lost Souls who still wander the Earth.

I will tell you that the Pleiadians have been molding the future of Earth for millions of years. They have not only been instrumental in the destruction of Mu, but also in allowing the Lizard People (i.e., the "Reptilians") to stay on Earth [as well].

Your Earth was not always a part of this solar system. It was created by the Demigods and brought to its present location by them. They were aware of the Pleiadians actions and knew the people of Mu needed a new home. [Because time as we know it does not exist in the higher dimensions] the Demigods knew the Pleiadians would be doing this and before it [even] happened, they had Earth ready.

The people of Mu made it to Earth and found it much like their old home [planet]. They landed on a large continent but saw that their population was such that even more land would be required. They sent out scouting parties and found many [other] places to dwell. The Earth had evolved past the time of dinosaurs and was now in the Pliocene era [5.3 to 1.8 million years ago]. There were primitive, ape-like beings, but the people of Mu did not interfere with them.

The planet Mu was a world of much beauty. It had many of the things that you enjoy on Earth. This being the case, visitors came from other worlds to see [the beauty] for themselves and also to talk to the human population.

Little Mu

Archangel Gabriel ⌒ Earth came in to being as a result of Mu's destruction. I am saying that part of Mu is still here in your Earth. Earth is Mu; the Demigods created Earth from particles of Mu and the consciousness of Mu. Instead of destroying its self again, this time the Earth *will* ascend. The people of Lemuria did not recognize the part of Earth that was Mu, but they did call themselves Lemurians in Mu's honor.

Lemurian Crystal ◡ The people of Mu called their new home Lemuria, which means "Little Mu". The Lemurian people continued to be loving and good. They spread over the face of the planet [Earth]. Many Star Brothers and Sisters came and mixed with them. They also altered their DNA and added some of their own [DNA]. This is how the many different races of Earth got their start. The races of the Stars have many humanoid forms, many of which are compatible with the people of Mu. The present inhabitants of Earth are not from this world at all—their ancestors came from many worlds. The Earth is a Living Library because your population contains DNA from so many Star races.

One population of Mu decided to live on a large island. They were very loving and intelligent. They had few wants—they lived simply. Their vibration was so high they no longer needed to eat. Then a few members of this community decided to investigate how it would feel to not be in such a high vibration. They wanted to experience Duality. God knew what would happen, but because this was a free will zone and God is a loving parent, he let the experiment proceed.

Atlantis

Lemurian Crystal ◡ These people became the Atlantians. They populated a new island and their culture was based on technology and power, not Love and Light. Atlantis is an ancient Mu word meaning "Enlightenment and Power".

The Lizard People came to Earth because they knew of the Atlantians. The planet Draconis [was at the time] home to a race of beings who [were] very war-like and not *of the Light*. They [were] always looking for planets to conquer and play havoc with. They were aware of the destruction of Mu and the flight of the population of Mu to Earth. This interested the Reptilians and they awaited an opportunity to cause trouble. The Reptilians not only influenced the Atlantians, they gave them technology [as well].

Reptilians and Annunaki

Ultimately, the rulers of Atlantis asked the Pleiadians, the *Keepers of the Living Library*, to allow them to try and manipulate the weather. For whatever reasons—the Pleiadians say they did not know at the time this would lead to the ultimate destruction of Atlantis and Lemuria—the Pleiadians granted them their request.

After the Atlantians were given the OK to proceed, they acquired technology from the Lizard People and later, from the Annunaki (who are *not* related to the Lizard People).

"ULTIMATELY, THE GREATEST MISTAKE THE ATLANTIANS MADE WAS TO BECOME ENSLAVED BY THEIR DESIRE FOR MORE AND MORE TECHNOLOGY."—*THE AUTHORS*

According to the Pleiadians, Atlantis existed for over one-hundred thousand years before it was destroyed and sank in to the ocean. Ultimately, the greatest mistake the Atlantians made was to become enslaved by their desire for more and more technology.

The Annunaki were also instrumental in the destruction of Maldek, the so-called "12th planet" of our solar system, according to Archangel Gabriel.

〜

Lemurian Crystal 〜 The people of Atlantis were very proud of their advancement. They had many wonderful devices that made their lives easy. They valued technology over Love and Spirituality. Because of this they looked at the Lemurian people with disdain and thought themselves better than they.

The Atlantians used Reptilian technology to dig deep into the ground looking for ways to disrupt water supplies to the Lemurian homes and fields. What they did not know was that a geothermal vent was near their dig site and they released so much energy that it started a chain-reaction that led to the breakup of their island [of Atlantis and the lands of Lemuria].

The Atlantians were now sorry they had listened to the Reptiles because their beautiful home was destroyed. They had to find new homes and they spread out over the face of the Earth and mingled with the other populations.

The Pleiadians *should have* seen that the Reptiles returned home, but they did not. In fact, they left Earth unprotected. The Reptiles took advantage of this and started planning how to control and take over the population of Earth. The [alien] Greys are not the only race who uses your people for their own desires and purposes—the Annunaki wish to have humans worship them[3].

"YOUR POWER IS THAT WHICH MAKES YOU INDEPENDENT. YOU GIVE YOUR POWER AWAY WHENEVER YOU LET OTHERS MAKE DECISIONS FOR YOU. YOUR GOVERNMENT HAS TAKEN MUCH POWER AWAY..."—*THE PLEIADIAN COLLECTIVE*[4]

The Reptiles are a race that does not value Love and Light as a whole. There are some exceptions but these are few. God is aware of them and wishes for them to learn and feel his Love. They have lessons to learn and will do so. They will watch as [Earth] ascends and much of the planet's population [as well].

Archangel Gabriel ⌒ The reptiles as a race have evolved and many are now peaceful and loving, however, those that came to Earth and remained to be involved in your culture are still war-like. When the Earth ascends these Reptiles will not be allowed to leave in [Star] ships; they will die and this will be a lesson to all who are not *of the Light*.

The people of Draconis are not all reptiles; some are dragons. The dragon race is very noble and loves being of Service To Others. A few heard of Earth and were curious about it, so they decided to teleport there and see it for themselves. Many of the dragons saw opportunities to serve and stayed on Earth.

The Pleiadian Collective ∼ We have heard you speaking to the Lemurian Crystal. We want you to know that the Pleiadian race has not abandoned its children. We have your best interests at heart.

The Lemurian Crystal ∼ The Pleiadians are a very old race. Their populations have long since given up Duality of any form; this including the male and female form. Therefore they reproduce in a manner totally different than anything you are used to. They are very self-absorbed and have a tendency not to involve themselves in the free will of others. The future of the Pleiadians rests not only with the Ascension of Humanity, but also with their ability to grow and become involved.

The Pleiadians

According to the Pleiadian Collective[‡], the Pleiadians were the original "librarians" of Mother Earth, in charge of what was and is known as the *Living Library*. This so-called library was not only filled with "knowledge" but was a store house for the DNA from many planets in this Universe. This makes sense since the Pleiadians were, and are, known as the greatest geneticists in the Universe. In reality, humans are the greatest "book" of DNA that exists in this Living Library.

∽

The Pleiadian Collective ∼ Your DNA is a combination of different Star DNA. The first human was not the ape man you are taught in your schools. The first human was one who came

----

‡   From the book, "2012 - Mother Earth Wants You!"

from the stars and was shown Earth and asked if they would like to live there.[5]

Telos

The people of Atlantis that did not die fled to other parts of the world. Some became people of wisdom. Many blended in with other human societies and lost their Atlantian heritage.

Some of the people of Lemuria that survived the castastrophy still dedicated themselves to living lives of Light and Love. They built a third-dimensional city called Telos, which was beautiful yet simple. They continued to love God and never doubted his greatness.

> **"There were, and are, other** *Middle Earth* **people under our surface. According to Archangel Gabriel, they are not Lemurian nor are they originally from Earth and they will ascend before the Earth does."**—*THE AUTHORS*

Because there was still negativity on Earth, the people of Telos decided to relocate the city inside Mount Shasta, in California. Using some of the ancient technologies they still possessed, but mostly with hard work, all traces of Telos were removed from the surface.

Within their Mount Shasta home the citizens of Telos continued to live with goodness and love in their hearts. Some became Masters and teachers. Some became the Keepers of the Sacred Temples. Some worked to help the people who still lived on the land to Awaken.

There were, and are, other *Middle Earth* people under our surface. According to Archangel Gabriel, they are "not Lemurian nor are they originally from Earth." Archangel Gabriel goes on to say, "the ones who are presently in Middle Earth are the descendents of the 'First People' and they *will* ascend before the Earth does."

Eventually the people of Telos and their beautiful city were rewarded with the gift of Ascension to the 5th dimension. Other Ascended Masters, like Lord Sananda and Saint Germain, joined the people of Telos because of the love and dedication and Service To Others these people had for the rest of humanity.

The people of Telos have not been the only beings on Earth to ascend. According to Archangel Gabriel, in regards to the Merpeople, "while most are still third-dimensional [and] *of the Light* (some are Neutral), many have Ascended."

"[T]he *Rites of Initiation* **were developed, not only as preparation for the Ascension Process but as a method to remove a Soul's karma..."**—*THE AUTHORS*

At some point, God again blessed the people of Telos and decided to give the Ascended Masters the job of helping not only humanity to Awaken, but to ascend as well. Thus the *Rites of Initiation* were developed, not only as preparation for the Ascension Process but as a method to remove a Soul's karma, which is necessary if one is to ascend.

Even now, as many of us on Earth look forward to our own Ascension to the 5th dimension, some of the Ascended Masters of Telos have begun their own Ascension into the 6th dimension.

~

Master Saint Germain ~ I am no longer in the 5th dimension, having Ascended to the 6th, but my concern for you has not changed. I see so many of you Awakening and it gladdens my heart. Keep up the good work! *

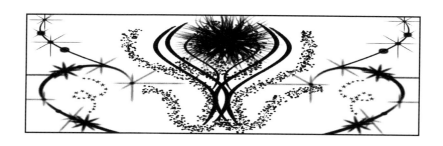

CHAPTER THREE

Why Are We Here?

Anahamar ⌣ We of Telos love all of humanity—no matter what your religion and no matter what color of your skin. We are all One and we are all Children of God.

Archangel Michael ⌣ We will speak of God's great gift to you. He has given [you] this opportunity to ascend. Not only does it break the need for your reincarnations, but it lets you take your body with you into the higher realms.

Millian ⌣ Believe it when we say this is a great gift from God. Never before has he allowed this to happen. Take advantage of this special opportunity and you will ascend in this lifetime.

> **"I NEVER INTENDED TO BECOME A CHURCH STARTER OR TO CAUSE RELIGIOUS WARS. HUMANITY DID NOT LISTEN TO THE TRUTH OF MY WORDS. THEY USED, I FEEL, WHAT THEY WANTED TO HEAR FOR THEIR OWN BENEFIT."** —*LORD SANANDA*

Lord Sananda ⌣ You are very special. As people on the Path to Ascension, your job is to become the best people you can be.

Lady Nada ⌣ You are very loved. Spread this love to all you meet.

Lord Sananda ⌣ I want you to know that we are closer to God here and we feel his love in every moment.

Adama ⌇ We will tell you why the people of Earth have taken so long to Awaken.

Lord Sananda ⌇ When I walked the Earth in human form, I came to teach people how to love. I never intended to become a church starter or to cause religious wars. Humanity did not listen to the Truth of my words. They used, I feel, what they wanted to hear for their own benefit.

Lady Nada ⌇ For thousands of years, mankind has suppressed Truth and kept it hidden—just as they have suppressed the female energies.

Sheylana ⌇ Now is the time for Truth to come out and be heard.

"IT IS A GREAT HONOR TO BE ALIVE AT THIS TIME. THIS IS WHY SO MANY CHILDREN ARE BEING BORN RIGHT NOW. EVEN IF THEY HAVE ONLY ONE OR TWO YEARS OF LIFE, THEY ARE A PART OF THE ASCENSION PROCESS..." —*LADY QUAN YIN*

Aurelia ⌇ What this means is that humanity will no longer be kept in the dark. We are revealing God's plan and how the forces of Darkness will finally be overcome.

Quan Yin ⌇ I will answer the question on how you will learn about the different ways in which you can meet your destiny. People of Earth came here during this time to be a part of the Ascension Process, whether for themselves or others.

It is a great honor to be alive at this time. This is why so many children are being born right now. Even if they have only one or two years of life, they are a part of the Ascension Process for humanity as a whole. Even if a person doesn't ascend they will have benefited in some way by being alive at this time. ✱

Prayer for Tree Blessing

I bless this tree
In the name of the Creator of All.
I give it energy, love and my protection.
I also say to all who you know,
That this day Lightworkers are now here
To reclaim the Light on Earth.

—Archangel Gabriel

Instructions

Create Blessed[6] or water "intended" with the nurturing energy of Earth Mother, the female aspect of God.

Apply some of this water to your finger or on the tree, and trace the Namaste REIKI symbol on the tree's bark, saying the *Tree Blessing* prayer from above.

If you are in the area, please bless the old-growth Redwood trees situated along the coast of Northern California.

Archangel Gabriel ⁓ The trees have protected Earth for millions of years. Your blessing them is a way to say "thank you" and to tell them that they are no longer alone in their job.

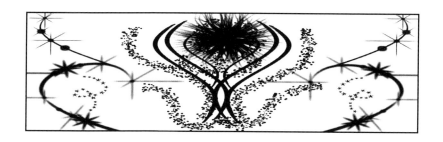

CHAPTER FOUR

Spiritual Growth

The history of planet Mu and its people is an example of the desire for all of God's creation to grow spiritually and evolve. Some take the high road and some take the low road; we don't all arrive at the same destination at once. Some, like the Lost Souls of Mu, can miscalculate and lose their Path.

Humanity, using its free will—under the guise of Duality and using the Veil as part of the support mechanism—has been involved in a spiritual experience that, according to Archangel Gabriel, "has never been allowed *anywhere* else." For many millennia we have supported Duality in various forms including war and peace, poverty and wealth, male versus female, Black vs. White, Service To Self and Service To Others, to name but a few. Humanity has stubbornly accepted Duality as our only reality.

"YOUR REALITY IS WHAT YOU MAKE OF IT." —*ADAMA*

Many have tried to overcome Duality and ascend during this shared experience; some have Awakened, but few have been chosen. Spiritual teachers such as Buddha and Jesus have come along to teach and serve as examples for living a life of Enlightenment, Love and Truth, but often their messages have become distorted, lost or only half-accepted.

According to Abraham[7] (the Celestial that interfaces between Mother Earth and humanity) the earth—our home—has longed for some time now to ascend. This process, which is not an easy one, can only occur once every 56 million years as the earth passes through a certain section of the Galaxy.

God has heard Mother Earth's prayers for Ascension during our current passage above the Galactic Center, and we should thank her for our opportunity to ascend, if we wish, as well. We also thank God for allowing all this to happen and thank the Ascended Masters for developing a Path to Ascension that we can follow as we try to grow spiritually in this lifetime.

⌒

Mother Mary ⌒ We want you to know that this Process of Ascension is a very special gift from God to humanity at this time.

Adama ⌒ Your reality is what you make of it.

Lord Sananda ⌒ I will speak about the need to believe; I want you to understand that it is your belief that motivates your reality.

Quan Yin ⌒ We also want you to know that many will ascend.

Reincarnation

The religions—and people—of our modern world differ in their belief of what happens after our physical bodies cease to function; some believe in reincarnation, some believe in resurrection and some believe that in death we cease to exist. Whether you currently accept the idea of reincarnation or not, the Ascended Masters teach that any thoughts of limited spiritual growth are an illusion; in truth we are all Divine beings, since we all retain a part of the One God that can exist for all eternity.

The Ascended Masters teach us that when we leave this life on Earth (whether by death or Ascension) we don't suddenly become the "perfect" Soul—there are hundreds of thousands of spiritual levels to aspire to as we search to become One with God. In essence we seek a Path back to God. Our desire is to evolve and seek paths that continually take us closer to God. While not all of these paths include incarnation, reincarnation on a third-dimensional world involving Duality and the Veil has been the fastest way for many Souls to grow.

When a Soul reincarnates it is for the benefit of spiritual advancement and includes lessons we may choose to learn and opportunities for growth during that incarnation. In reincarnation however, versus Ascension, you create a new "you" each time based on your Soul's unique vibration and as appropriate for the life you are being born into. With few exceptions, there are no reincarnations in the 5th dimension and above; Souls can advance spiritually by being Angels, Spirit Guides, working in the various Temples, etc.

$$\backsim$$

Lady Nada ⌐ We will speak today of your life's journey. You were born to learn and grow spiritually. Every time you reincarnate you have a list of lessons you wish to learn about. You ask members of your Soul Family to play parts in your life and to be born around the same time so you can interact.

Quan Yin ⌐ We will speak now of why you continually reincarnate. Sometimes the lessons you come to learn are not accomplished: you could not complete your mission or you lost your true path. This causes much pain and sadness and you accumulate karma.

Mother Mary ⌐ When your life is over, you have a chance to review it's journey. You then get to decide if you have more to accomplish. If you desire to try again, you reincarnate as many times as it takes until all the lessons are learned.

The Lemurian Crystal ⌒ I have a happy story: I knew a family in Lemuria which consisted of a mother, father and several children. During the breakup of the islands, this family became scattered. One of the children became lost and eventually died. This child was determined to be reunited with her family and so kept reincarnating through countless lives until one life she Awoke and grew [as a Lightworker] so much her light could be seen from [outer] space.

Duality and the Veil

Aurelia ⌒ I wish to speak about the experience of being on the other side. When you die it is not a true "death" because you still exist. The many religions of the world talk about reincarnation and it is only part of the story. We reincarnate to learn and grow, but also to ascend. The goal is to raise your vibrational energy to the next highest level. So when we die, there is no such thing as death—we just change form.

> **"I CAN TELL YOU, THAT UNTIL YOU GET OFF THIS PLANET, THINGS ARE GOING TO BOTHER YOU. YOU ARE GOING TO HAVE BAD DAYS, GOOD DAYS... WHAT I WANT YOU TO SEE IS THAT THIS [LIFE] IS A CLASSROOM, IT'S NOT REAL—YOU'VE CREATED IT... THE DRAWBACK IS THAT YOU BOUGHT IT—YOU MADE THIS ILLUSION MORE REAL THAN YOU CAN POSSIBLY IMAGINE."**
> —*BENU (CHANNELED BY KAREN COOK)*[8]

Lord Hilarion ⌒ My wish is for you to know how greatly we admire those who ask for our help. To Awaken from the dream of Duality and the illusion of separation is a marvelous thing and we rejoice with you.

Lord Sananda ⌒ We of Telos have seen humanity struggle with Duality and we know this lesson [of Duality] is about over.

Aurelia ⌒ I wish to answer the question about your need for a Light being's [(Spirit Guide)] help. Humans come into life with no memory of their True Self and they also have the Veil. The Veil is something which keeps you from seeing a person in another dimension or "ghosts".

Adama also says that the Veil is God's way of protecting the human mind from experiencing things that it couldn't understand or would be frightened of. There are some individuals, who because of their Divine Contracts, have less of a Veil than others. Humans [because of Duality and the Veil] need Light beings to help them because they go through life feeling alone and cut off from the Universe.

Mother Mary ⌒ I will answer the question on "when will [we] see ghosts?" The three hours of Darkness will come near the end of 2012 but not too close to Ascension. It will be a time when you will have the Veil lifted and all will see [those in the 4th and higher dimensions].

Why Ascend?

Sheylana ⌒ We will talk about why you would want to ascend. Once your body leaves the 3rd dimension it no longer has limitations. By this I mean there is no sickness, no death as you know it, no need to eat if you do not wish to, nor do you have to worry about any of your daily habits. Your body will be perfect in every way and you can improve any feature you wish.

Ascended Masters ⌒ We also wish to point out that the Universe on a whole is always growing and in a million years, there could be many more dimensions added. God is such a wonderful parent that he wants all his children to be happy.

The Other Kingdoms*

Most of humanity continues to believe they are the dominant species on this planet. Yet even your family pet or the tree in your yard are part of the Other Kingdoms. Tales of dragons, fairies, elves, gnomes etcetera exist in children's stories and are told as fables and myth. The same applies to sentient life on other planets. People who speak of alien encounters are ridiculed and made fun of.

Yet now is the time for humanity to learn the Truth and Awaken. Humans are but one form of life that exists on this planet and in the cosmos. Many of these races, beings and entities live in a higher vibrational state (dimension) than we do. While this may make them currently "invisible" to the average human, it does not make them any less real. ✻

> **"ASCENSION IS SOMETHING OPEN TO ALL OF CREATION—NOT JUST HUMANS. YOUR FAMILY PET CAN ALSO ASCEND, IF THAT IS ITS WISH. WE WANT TO TELL YOU THAT THE ASCENSION PROCESS IS THE SAME FOR ALL NO MATTER WHAT YOU ARE: HUMAN, TREE, ANIMAL OR EVEN THE EARTH HERSELF."**—*ASCENDED MASTERS*

Ascended Masters ⌢ We have many things to tell you, not only about the Ascension Process for humans, but how it will affect the Other Kingdoms as well. We have been thinking about how best to explain this in terms all will understand. You see, Ascension is something open to all of Creation—not just humans. Your family pet can also ascend, if that is its wish. We want to tell you that the Ascension Process is the same for all no matter what you are: human, tree, animal or even the Earth herself.

---

*   For more information read the book, "The Other Kingdoms Speak Out".

Adama ⌒ Not only is it available to everyone, but to all King-doms as well. Many are not aware that they share this world with more than humanity. I will tell you that there are many beings who you cannot see, but who you know as "fairy tales". These beings are real and they are loved by God as much as humans are.

Sara (the Dragon) ⌒ My planet is Draconis, but I live on Earth. I know of the Earth Changes and will stay to witness the events as they unfold. Eventually I plan to ascend before the Earth does.

I have been preparing for my Ascension in the same way a human does. I have been taught by the Ascended Masters and I have undergone the *Rites of Initiation*. Everyone is able to ask for this process—it is not just for humans.

Be aware that your time is short: if you want to ascend you must start the process soon. All you have to do is ask. I will see you on the other side.

> **"It is my mission to assist humanity, especially during this period of Earth Ascension. You can believe or not, but these things are true and much will come to pass that will have you in fear. My message is to have faith and to believe not only in all the King-doms but also in God..."**—ARCHANGEL MICHAEL[9]

Andracian (from Draconis) ⌒ We come to Earth now because of its Ascension. The time grows short and there is much work to be done by those who wish to Awaken. You must realize that your world is more than you can see. The Other Kingdoms await your Awakening. My people know that you are just beginning to become aware of our presence. If you hope to ascend before the Earth's Ascension you must get busy. There is not much time left. Many races watch from orbit to see what the humans of Earth will do or how many will Awaken in time.

Cinobar (the Dragon) ⌒ I am from the planet Percides. My friends and I want you to know that the Dragon People on Earth are aware that the Earth Changes start soon. We will do our best to lead humans to safety, if they will listen to us.

We can whisper in their ears or—for those that can see us—we will lead them to places of safety. As the Earth starts her Ascension, many of us will return home. Some will go to Earth2 and others will await the reincarnation of Earth1. It is to be a great event and we will do our part.

Andracian (from Draconis) ⌒ My people are what you call lizard-like, but many of us are *of the Light*. On my home planet there are Dragon people as well as Lizard People. We know of Earth because many of us travel here to visit the Other Kingdoms that exist along with humanity. If you only knew how many dragons and fairy people you had on your planet you would be surprised.

> **"THOSE WHO HAVE COME FROM OTHER PLANETS AND LIVE ON EARTH MAY ALSO ASCEND IF THEY WORK HARD AND ASK FOR THE RITES OF INITIATION. WE MAKE NO DISTINCTION." —MASTER SAINT GERMAIN**

Master Saint Germain ⌒ All Kingdoms may ascend. Dragons born on Earth have Soul Contracts that tie them to Earth and they can ascend in the Mass Ascension if they prepare. Those who have come from other planets and live on Earth [now] may also ascend if they work hard and ask for the Rites of Initiation. We make no distinction.

Archangel Gabriel ⌒ If a dragon who is not from Earth does not want to ask for the *Rites* [of Ascension] they can go to their home [planet]. If a dragon born on Earth does not ask for the Rites they will go to Earth2 but [will] remain in the same dimension and level [as they are now]. The reason a [fifth-dimensional] dragon born on Earth would want to ascend is to go to a higher dimension level within their present dimension. ✳

Blessing God's Creatures

I bless this creature of God's creation.
I give it energy, love and protection.
I also grant that all who know this creature,
Will testify that it has been blessed
By a Lightworker today.

—Archangel Raphael

Instructions

If possible, create water "intended" with the nurturing energy of Earth Mother, the female aspect of God.

If possible, apply some of this water to your finger and trace the Namaste Reiki symbol on the creature, saying the *Blessing God's Creatures* prayer from above.

Else, from afar, trace the Namaste Reiki symbol at the creature, saying the *Blessing God's Creatures* prayer.

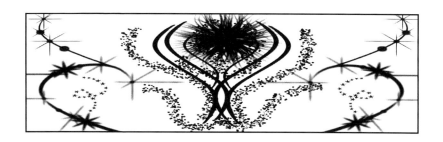

CHAPTER FIVE

The Path to Ascension

Anahamar ⌒ To ascend means to go from your 3rd dimension to a higher one. This process uses cosmic energy. As your Earth approaches a new section of the Universe it will pass through a very special energy field. This field has the potential to excite the atoms of your body in a spectacular way. Those who have been attuning to all the new energies coming to Earth will find this an easy transition.

Lady Nada ⌒ We will be explaining more on each of these steps as we progress and your understanding is expanded. For now, we will keep it simple, but do not worry—all will be revealed before your time to ascend.

Ascended Masters ⌒ God has never before allowed so many to ascend at once, the reason being that Ascension had to be earned. In his great love for both humanity and Mother Earth, he has given this opportunity to all of his children on Earth—not only humans, but also the Other Kingdoms as well. God loves us all and has seen how you have struggled with the lessons of Duality. He also loves your planet very much and has heard her prayers to ascend.

The planet you call Earth is really a sentient being that feels and has thoughts. For millions of years she has waited for the opportunity to be in the center of the Universe where the energies will allow for her Ascension. God has heard her prayers and this time she will ascend. All life on her surface will either ascend or go elsewhere to continue their learning.

We believe that humanity has been given a great gift that has never been given before in all of recorded time. Those who are Awakened and take the opportunities presented—like the *Rites of Initiation*—will be allowed to ascend.

God has given the Ascended Masters the task of teaching those who wish to ascend because it is not something that can be done without preparation, both in body and spiritually.

"THE ASCENSION PROCESS IS NOT SOMETHING THAT SHOULD BE TAKEN LIGHTLY. YOU HAVE TO WANT TO ASCEND FOR ALL THE RIGHT REASONS AND ONLY YOU CAN TELL WHAT THOSE REASONS ARE." —LORD SANANDA

Lord Sananda ⌒ The Ascension Process is not something that should be taken lightly. You have to want to ascend for all the right reasons and only you can tell what those reasons are.

Adama ⌒ I wish to speak of why you would want to ascend. Not only do you take your body with you but you can improve it.

Sheylana ⌒ We have spoken of this before but what we did not mention was the many choices open to you.

Lord Sananda ⌒ In the 5th dimension you are not here just to relax but to continue being of Service. This means learning and growing spiritually.

Mother Mary ⌒ You will be allowed to work in the Temples, become Guardian Angels or Spirit Guides. You may also become a student of one of the Masters and study under them.

Quan Yin ⌒ I have to add that many will be surprised at all there is to do here. We do not work all the time.

Aurelia ⌒ The 5ᵗʰ dimension takes some getting used to and we will help you adjust. We will be with you and advise you on anything you care to ask. No one is forced to do anything. They have complete control of what they want to do. When you elevate yourself to the 5ᵗʰ dimension your way of thinking and being is totally changed. You are no longer worried about the same concerns or problems [as you worry about now].

Master Saint Germain ⌒ I will add that in the higher realms your Soul shines and your spirit is free from worries. There are no bills to pay, deadlines to meet or bosses to worry about. Growth and learning happen at a rate comfortable to each individual. You are never forced to do anything—you are so loved by God that he wants you to be happy always.

God ⌒ Be it known that you are greatly loved and that this is my beloved Chosen One in whom I am well pleased. Hear the words written here and know that time is growing short. You must Awaken soon or you will not ascend.

Becoming

The process of Becoming is not something that happens overnight, but rather requires commitment and perseverance. You have to want to change in body, mind and spirit. In body, not only will you change on a cellular level but in eating habits as well. In mind, you will change not only how you think about the world, but how you perceive yourself and others. In Spirit, you will feel a part of the One and learn to shine your Light for all the world to see. Friends and family may not understand or be aware of your commitment to Become; this is a time when many may choose paths that separate them from friends and family.

⌒

Aurelia ⌒ We will talk about your need to Become.

Lord Sananda ⌒ Today is a wonderful day because we will talk of how you will "Become".

Sheylana ⌒ We want you to know that the Path to Ascension and Becoming is one in which you will find not only your life, but also yourself, changing. First, change your attitude to one of love. Second, change your body by proper food choices and third, change your world by shining your Light for all to see.

Lady Nada ⌒ "Becoming" is a process where you begin to understand that all things are part of the One.

Millian ⌒ To prepare your bodies to tolerate the energies coming to Earth you need to begin now. This means changing many of your old habits.

"Those of you who are meat eaters will find your taste for meat changing. Eating more vegetables in as natural a state as possible is the best."
—*MILLIAN, THE ASCENDED MASTER*

Those of you who are meat eaters will find your taste for meat changing. Eating more vegetables in as natural a state as possible is the best. Also, drink less coffee and caffeinated beverages. Drink instead pure water from the Earth and not distilled which takes out the minerals.

Remember to bless your food and intend it to be healthy for your body. If you do this, not only will it do your body more good, but it will also take out unwanted calories. This does not mean you should go on a dessert binge, however. Remember: the key to good health is balance and moderation. Lastly, get enough rest and thank the Universe each morning for another day of life.

Lady Nada ⌒ It is not only the body that will undergo changes, but also your spirit. The I AM Presence will merge with your body and join in a union of body and soul. You will remember your divinity and your [true] heritage. You will remember your past lives and not be afraid of them. All of your karmic debt will have been cleared by then.

Aurelia ⌒ You may wonder why we speak to you from our place here in Telos. We are soon to meet you in person, but that can only happen when your vibration has raised enough so you can see us.

Sheylana ⌒ We will talk about how to be more loving. The Ascension Process cannot occur if you do not know how to love. This means unconditional love, for not only your fellow humans, but the other Kingdoms as well.

Aurelia ⌒ We mean to tell you that love is for everyone and not just your family members, but those who you don't know—yes, even the stranger on the street corner. You don't have to leave them your money or show them your home, but you can love the spark of God within them.

"You do not have to condone improper behavior, but you must recognize the spark of God within them and love that."—*Lady Quan Yin*

Adama ⌒ Love is your heritage. God's love is unconditional. It knows no boundaries: not color, race, social order or wealth.

Hilarion ⌒ We will speak now of what you need to do to become more loving.

Quan Yin ⌒ We say the word "love" so often it has lost its true meaning: to "love" is to accept. You love someone when you accept them for who they are and still know they are children of God. You do not have to condone improper behavior, but you must recognize the spark of God within them and love that.

Mother Mary ⌒ It is easy for a mother to love her children. It is not always easy to love those who hurt our children, but those who hurt others are someone's children and they are loved by a mother somewhere.

Lord Sananda ⌒ Love is a necessary ingredient for the Ascension Process. It fits in with being in a higher vibrational state, because love itself is a high vibrational energy.

Millian ⌒ Love is your gift to the world. Share the energy of love to all you come in contact with. In doing so you will raise the vibrational frequency of the world and when the frequency of the world increases, more people will Awaken to the Ascension Process.

Lady Nada ⌒ Love is more than just sexual in nature. You must have love for all life and realize that God is present in all life, if you wish to become Light.

"Spread your light and you will see your world change before your eyes. It all begins in your own heart with love." —*MILLIAN, AN ASCENDED MASTER*

Lord Lanto ⌒ Wisdom and Light are yours if you only take the time to meditate and grow. Light is the absence of Dark thoughts.

Archangel Gabriel ⌒ Love must indeed spread across your planet if the negative energy is to be transformed into a higher vibration.

Saint Germain ⌒ Your Lightworkers are doing a wonderful job of letting love spread. Keep up the good work and remember to imagine how you want your world to be. Remember to imagine a kinder, more loving world and it will become your reality.

Millian ⌒ I think Master Saint Germain is correct. You must start thinking about how you want your world to become and then behave as if it were that way. Be more loving. Spread your Light and you will see your world change before your eyes. It all begins in your own heart with love.

Aurelia ⌒ We are speaking of treating all living things with the respect they deserve because they are all part of God's creation.

Saint Germain ⌒ You are so very loved. Remember to love others the same way.

Quan Yin ⌒ Not only must you love your fellow human, but the animals, plants and insects around you because they are part of the "One" also.

Mother Mary ⌒ You must learn to love with your whole heart and being. This means not just when things are easy, but also when you have been hurt by others. You must see the face of God reflected back at you when you look out into the world. Treat all that you see with the same respect you would give to God and yourself.

"YOUR LIFE SHOULD REFLECT YOUR NEW INTENTIONS. YOU CANNOT ACT THE SAME WAY AS YOU DID BEFORE BECAUSE NOW YOU ARE AWAKENED AND MUST LIVE TO A HIGHER SET OF STANDARDS." —*LADY NADA*

Lord Sananda ⌒ You can "Become".

Lady Nada — Your life should reflect your new intentions. You cannot act the same way as you did before because now you are Awakened and must live to a higher set of standards.

Lord Sananda ⌒ Trust that your life will unfold in wondrous ways and you will be a happier, more peaceful person.

Saint Germain ⌒ I want to tell you that once you start on this Path you will never be the same—you will be better. You become the best person you can be.

Quan Yin ⌒ I wish to say only that a person on the Path to Ascension is a more loving, kind and compassionate person.

Aurelia ⌒ Learning to love someone who hurts us does not mean we condone their actions; it means we love the God Spark within them.

Mother Mary ⌒ We mean to say that you will become more Christ-like.

God ⌒ My message is for you to see yourselves as representatives of my chosen people here on Earth and become examples for the world. By your actions and loving examples will you be known.

Adama ⌒ You should also learn to talk to God. I wish to explain about how to speak to God. You do not need a church because God is everywhere. I want you to believe that whenever you speak, God hears you. I also want you to make your life a continual prayer to God. This means being your best at all times, not just when you walk into a church or holy place.

You are going to find that [talking to God] has an enormous change in your daily life. When you change your attitude from one of negativity to one of love and gratitude, you will change yourself in ways beyond measure.

**"LOOK UPON THE WORLD WITH EYES OF LOVE
AND HAVE COMPASSION FOR THOSE WHO HAVE YET
TO DISCOVER THIS TRUTH." —*LADY QUAN YIN***

Lord Sananda ⌒ I want you to know that inner peace is achievable by all. You do not have to have a degree in theology or be a nun. Inner peace is knowing that you are loved by God for yourself and all your imperfections.

Lady Nada ⌒ I want you to know that it does not matter what other people think of you. It is what you know in your heart that counts.

Lady Quan Yin ⌒ Compassion is yours, but you must use it daily. Do not keep it just for yourself. Look upon the world with eyes of love and have compassion for those who have yet to discover this truth.

Aurelia ⌒ Your questions will be many, but let me say this. Start by allowing yourself time to absorb all the information. Don't worry about getting it all right now. Start with just thinking about your life and how you could improve it with a change of attitude here or there. Let that work for a while and see if you don't see a change for the better. And when I say work, I mean honestly try. It will be the start of your journey toward Ascension.

Adama ⌒ The [Ascension] Process is quite long but also it is very easy. What I mean is this: you have much work to do on a spiritual and physical level, but the actual Ascension process itself is over in seconds.

Love and Happiness

Adama ⌒ I will speak on the subject of love and happiness. To ascend, one must learn how to be happy and keep their thoughts from being negative. The higher dimensions are places of great love and the vibration of these realms are such that one must have pure thoughts.

"I BELIEVE YOUR THOUGHTS ARE NEGATIVE WHEN THEY HAVE NO LOVE IN THEM. I ALSO KNOW THAT GOD IS ALWAYS LISTENING AND WILL BE THE JUDGE OF ALL." —*LORD SANANDA*

Sheylana ⌒ We can speak of what is in our hearts and know that there are no shadows—only Love and Light.

Lady Nada ⌒ I will add that even those who are of the "Dark" do not have negative thoughts. This may seem like a contradiction, but it is true.

Lord Sananda ⌒ I believe your thoughts are negative when they have no love in them. I also know that God is always listening and will be the judge of all.

Tests of Discernment and Light

The Earth is a classroom. There have always been tests to see how far we have progressed spiritually. Some of these tests involve our faith in God, our belief in our own abilities including intuition, our connections to our Higher Selves and Spirit Guides, our connections to Other Kingdoms, and our ability to validate and discern outside information, among other things.

Not everyone is going to ascend. As Jesus was quoted as saying, in the Bible, "Many are called, but few are chosen." It means that God calls everyone and gives them the power to respond, but to be chosen—to ascend—we must respond to the call; we must "Become", if you will, using the power God gave us for that purpose.

Planet X

Sheylana ⁓ I will address your concerns over the coming of a planet [into our Solar system]. There is indeed a planet approaching Earth that has negative entities on it. They will stop outside your planet's orbit and observe. They would like to use Earth as a place to spread their negativity. It is the job of you Lightworkers to shine your love so strongly that its Light can be seen from space. This will discourage these entities from wanting to try anything.

Archangel Gabriel ⁓ This is a planet of negative Reptilians in the 3rd dimension.

Quan Yin ⌒ I will add that being "of the Dark" is not the same as being "evil".

Mother Mary ⌒ I have this to add: you are beings of Light; act as such and your ability to ascend will be assured.

Aurelia ⌒ You will probably want to know how a being *of the Dark* can still be loving and not evil. Our minds give the wrong connotation to "evil". Darkness means they have cut themselves off from the Love of God. It does not mean that they are evil. There is no evil in the higher dimensions.

"Understand that learning and growing continues even in the higher dimensions. A being can still make mistakes and judge themselves unworthy of love from God." —ASCENDED MASTER SHEYLANA

Adama ⌒ I will talk about how you can become more loving. To "love" does not mean in a sexual way but rather in a Divine way. If you can find the God in others and love that part, then you are [placing yourself] in a higher vibration. Those who do not allow this cut themselves off from love.

Those in the higher dimensions who are *of the Dark* do not let God's love reach them. While they vibrate to a higher frequency, their love is stunted and does not shine for all to see. We pray for Souls such as these so they will eventually accept God's Love and become like love themselves. These Souls are not evil. True evil does not exist in the higher dimensions. *True evil is a concentration of such negativity that it takes on a form and has an awareness.*

Sheylana ⌒ A "Neutral" entity is one who is unsure of their beliefs. They do not allow themselves to feel God's love, but they believe in God. There is no advantage to this—only sadness, for one does not rejoice in God's Love. A Soul cuts themselves off from God because they do not feel they are worthy of his love.

Yes—they feel unworthy of his love because of something they have not forgiven themselves for.

Understand that learning and growing continues even in the higher dimensions. A [higher dimension] being can still make mistakes and judge themselves unworthy of love from God. I think that prayer is always a good idea even when we feel God's love and especially for those who don't.

Millian ⌒ I will speak about incorporating more Light into not only your meditations, but your life. Let's start with meditating. You should try and do this each and every day. Meditation can be as simple as sitting beneath a tree or watching nature or it can be a ritual of deep breathing and letting the mind quiet. Whatever form you choose, see yourself as Light and be happy in your meditations. This brings you less stress and your Light will shine from your being and lift up anyone who comes close to you.

"People who start on their Path toward Ascension are also likely to lose friends. This is because they see the world differently now..." —LORD SANANDA

Adama ⌒ We will speak on the role of Ascension in your daily life and by that, I mean how being on the Path to Ascension changes how you live. No one who wishes to ascend can be on their Path and not be changed by it. The changes will be for the good of the person, but it does often come as a shock to others in their life. For example, a meat eater may, all of a sudden, become a vegetarian. Or a coffee drinker may cut out drinking coffee. These are small changes, but [they] may be looked upon as strange by others.

Lord Sananda ⌒ People who start on their Path toward Ascension are also likely to lose friends. This is because they see the world differently now and their opinions about things change, but those of their friends do not.

Lady Nada ⌒ Life is not always easy for those on the Ascension Path. You are tested by the Angels and questioned by God.

Mother Mary ⌒ I wish to tell you that the Ascended Masters only want you to realize what a big commitment this is and not to take it lightly.

Quan Yin ⌒ We of Telos also want you to know that we love you and applaud your decision to start on this Path.

Sheylana ⌒ I will say that all who choose this Path will be given all the help they need.

Aurelia ⌒ I just want you to understand that what the Ascended Masters are trying to tell you is this is not something that you just sign up for and you are done. It requires work on your part.

> **"AS FOR WHY TELOS WAS CHOSEN, IT WAS BECAUSE LONG AGO THEY PROVED THROUGH THEIR LOVE AND DEVOTION TO GOD THAT THEY WERE WORTHY OF SUCH A TASK."** —*LORD SANANDA*

Lord Sananda ⌒ If someone asks why they need to go through the *Rites of Initiation* or why the people of Telos get to decide who is worthy of Ascension, say to them, "*God has decreed that this is how it will be.*" This is such a great opportunity and it is God's Will that it be done this way.

As for why Telos was chosen, it was because long ago they proved through their love and devotion to God that they were worthy of such a task.

I became associated with Telos because of my desire to also help humanity at this time.

Not Becoming

One of the reasons for spreading the Light of understanding is so those who may be lagging behind can respond to it and have the same opportunities for Ascension as every one else. As always, it is their choice—the pace of spiritual progress is not imposed upon any Soul. Some humans hardly ever question the purpose of their Life; many of these are so lacking in awareness that it is difficult to Awaken them. Life is about taking responsibility for yourself and others and progress can be measured by how much your love spreads to all life forms.

Evolving spiritually towards Ascension is not always easy, but we proceed at our own pace and with true intent, one cannot fail to eventually be successful. While many humans may be on "autopilot" their lives still follow a Path often decided upon by their Guides, who continually arrange experiences that satisfy their Soul Contracts and offer opportunities to open their eyes towards enlightenment.

Even though their Spirit Guides and Guardians are always trying to lead these Souls towards the Light, many will choose to "leave" early to reside in the Astral realm where they can take their time in deciding when and where next to incarnate. They can meet up with their loved ones and friends in the higher dimensions if they are sufficiently advanced spiritually or if not, they can choose to incarnate into a similar level to where they left off, to allow for further evolution appropriate to the experiences required to do so.

～

Adama ～ I would like to answer the question about why some are chosen and others are not. I want to tell you that all who ask for learning are given all that they need, but it is also up to them to do much work on both a spiritual and a physical level. This is not something all are willing to do. You cannot ascend if your body and spirit are not totally prepared.

Blessing God's Children

I bless this person
In the name of the Creator of All.
Let it be known that this day
A Lightworker has blessed and gifted
Their Love, Energy and Protection
To this person.

—Archangel Raphael

Instructions

If possible, create water "intended" with the nurturing energy of Earth Mother, the female aspect of God.

If possible, apply some of this water to your finger and trace the Namaste Reiki symbol on the person, saying the *Blessing God's Children* prayer from above.

Else, from afar, trace the Namaste Reiki symbol at the person, saying the *Blessing God's Children* prayer.

Archangel Raphael ⌣ People need blessing too, especially children. When you bless something [or someone] you are actually giving to them the God Energy gifted to you as Lightworkers.

Anahamar ⌒ Not all will ascend. Those who have not prepared will feel extremely uncomfortable and some may even decide to pass from their lives. Know that all will be taken care of and if they don't ascend in this life, they can reincarnate [on a different third-dimensional planet] to try again.

Lord Sananda ⌒ I will speak about what happens to those who die before they ascend. Like our beautiful Aurelia, many people will pass over to our side before the Great Ascension. This does not mean they will not have a chance to ever ascend. It only means that their journey will be longer and that they will ascend in another lifetime.

Ascended Masters ⌒ We can tell you that much life on Earth will ascend in 2012. We see that you think of those who will remain and yes, they will notice that something has happened. They will not understand, but they will see that you are no longer around. Those who do not ascend will eventually die before the Earth herself ascends.

Sheylana ⌒ I want to talk about how the Ascension Process will be felt by those who do *not* ascend. Everyone on Earth will be affected by the [Ascension] energies, but only those who have prepared for the Ascension Process will ascend.

Those who are not going to ascend will still feel the energy and it will make them somewhat uncomfortable. They will have the cells of their bodies vibrate, but they will not have those cells drift apart—nor will they become less dense. This will cause some discomfort and some pain but will not kill them.

I think that those who do not ascend will see the Ascension of all the others and understand that something major is happening. You will be able to physically see the Ascension Process, so those who are not Ascending will witness an amazing event. I believe that those who do not ascend will soon realize that they have missed out on an opportunity and will regret being left behind.

THE PATH TO ASCENSION

I will also mention that just because they did not ascend this time does not mean they cannot still work towards that goal. They will be given the opportunity to reincarnate and continue to grow and learn and work their way toward [a future] Ascension.

I will address some concerns I am sure you must have about family and friends. You may want to know if they will notice you are gone once you ascend. The answer is "yes". Your house will be there but you will be nowhere to be found. There will be lots of questions asked because so many people will have gone missing at once.

Some will ascend in a public place and there will be witnesses to the event. Those left behind will begin to understand that they have missed a great opportunity. Do not worry! God loves them and will see that they are given every opportunity to reincarnate and continue to grow spiritually so that they too can eventually ascend.

I will speak about your right to choose. After your life on Earth has ended, you always have the opportunity to live again. This is why even those who do not ascend in this lifetime are not to be forgotten or left behind. They will continue to work towards that goal.

Aurelia ⌒ Many of you know that I did not ascend. This was my choice, but do not feel sad for me. I have been given so much love and have so many friends and family on this side that I am very happy.

Millian ⌒ I will be here to welcome all who do not ascend, but die. Do not worry about those who pass over because they will always be given more chances for continual [spiritual] growth and to ascend at another time.

Aurelia ⌒ I also want to tell you humanity will not long survive on Earth past the Ascension date because the Earth herself will be going through some of the more violent [Earth] changes that must occur before she ascends. I can also say that everyone will be given all the opportunities and help necessary to become ready for the Ascension Process.

Adama 〜 The Ascension Process is our main concern, but not our only concern. Since not all will ascend, we need to have some information for those who do not want to ascend or [those who] don't believe. These people need to understand what awaits them. Their fate will be an uncomfortable one.

Because the energies coming to Earth during that time when [the] masses ascend will be of such magnitude, those whose bodies have not prepared will feel much discomfort; they will feel like they are being compressed. This is not actually the case nor will they die from the experience itself but many will decide to pass during this time.

Those who remain after the Mass Ascension will be left on an empty earth. Many plants and animals will ascend also. It will not be the same Earth as you now enjoy. I say this only as a warning to those who will be left behind [i.e., those who choose not to ascend].

Lord Sananda 〜 I can tell those who do not ascend that they will not be forgotten by God. They will have the chance to ascend in another life, but they will not live much longer on this earth.

Mother Mary 〜 I want you not to worry about your other family members. All will be welcomed to the other side and greeted by us; we will ease the transition of death.

I want you to know that I too felt the loss of a child and it was great sorrow, but in the end, we were reunited and have been together ever since.

Lady Quan Yin 〜 We love all the brave Souls who are on Earth at this time and whether you ascend or not, our help will be there when you need it.

Lady Nada ⌒ I want you to know that you will realize what a great opportunity you missed out on and when you cry out in despair we will hear you and comfort you.

Master Saint Germain ⌒ It is my honor to tell you that all of the people of Earth are looked upon as brave Souls. You are not only going through some upsetting times and changes, but you are conquering the Darkness with your Light. Even if you don't ascend this time you will be given other chances. We will still be here to teach you and help you learn.

Aurelia ⌒ It is my pleasure to tell you that I am among those who will be given a second chance at life. I will help all who pass over to see that they are not alone in their journey.

Adama ⌒ We will speak of why some will not ascend. If a person does not ask for the *Rites of Ascension* they cannot ascend. This may seem harsh but you must understand that the higher realms are places where there is purity and no karma.

Lord Sananda ⌒ It is karma that you must rid yourself of and from not just this life, but all your past lives as well.

Lady Nada ⌒ I will tell you that even if you [currently] lead a good life it does not remove karma—this can only be accomplished through help at the various Temples.

Mother Mary ⌒ We know that many religions do not believe in reincarnation. This will be hard for many to accept.

Quan Yin ⌒ We of Telos are here to tell you that your religious leaders have taught what they believed to be Truth, but they were wrong. Life is for learning and more lives mean more learning.

Aurelia ⌒ I wish to add that even those who believe in reincarnation may still have problems believing in the need to ask the Ascended Masters for help. ✳

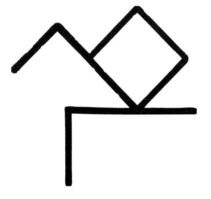

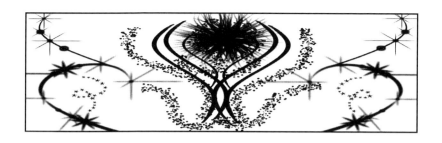

CHAPTER SIX

Ascension Requirements

Aurelia 〜 Many will ask why we come to you at this point in time with talk of Ascension. My friends, the time is very short—you have but a few years to make yourselves ready.

Mother Mary 〜 Our children will be with us and they will love us as we love them.

Adama 〜 I wish to speak about the importance of asking questions. The Ascension Process will be a long road and one on which you will do much learning. It is also a journey through your own mind. You will be taught and you will be tested.

You are allowed to ask questions, for that is how you learn. We may not always answer in ways that you expect or understand immediately, but you will find that our answers cause you to think and eventually, grow in mind and spirit.

Mother Mary 〜 We of Telos want you to know that you cannot fail, nor believe too much or not enough.

Requesting the Rites

Anahamar 〜 We will speak of your Ascension Process. It all starts with your intention. You have to want to ascend and you must ask for the *Rites of Initiation*.

Lord Sananda ⌒ To those who would ask why these Initiations are necessary, we would say, "At each Temple you are not only being taught, but also your karma is lifted." This karma is from this life as well as past lives. No one can ascend unless they are karma free. *I can truthfully tell you that no karma is ever removed unless it is done in the Temples.*

I can tell... that people are not believing the need to come to the Temples. Karma is the leftover energy that results from acts done during a lifetime [past or current]... People need to come to the Temples [because] karma can be deeply embedded within a person's etheric bodies and the attachment [can be] extremely difficult to sever.

I have much to say about your desire to ascend. First, ask us to teach you each night as you sleep. Then make your thoughts one of love and graditude.

"The request to start the Rites can be as simple as praying, *In the name of the God within me 'I AM', I ask to receive the initiations needed to qualify for Ascension.*" —*ASCENDED MASTERS*[10]

Adama ⌒ You must be given lessons in the many *Temples of the Seven Rays* if you wish to ascend.

Mother Mary ⌒ We want you to know you must ask for these lessons and set your intentions to join us. Your Guides can take your mental body to Telos where the Masters will teach you.

Hilarian ⌒ We also want you to know that anyone who wishes to learn will be invited: we do not make any restrictions about who can receive instructions. People from all walks of life and any religion are welcome.

As you pass each initiation, you go on to the next temple where you learn more until you have passed that initiation and so on.

Saint Germain ⌢ As you continue, your karmic debt is released and you are able to let go of all your past lives and concentrate on this life. You will find yourself changing not only in your attitude towards life but in how you deal with other people as well.

Lord Sananda ⌢ Your life will become fuller and you will be happier.

Lady Nada ⌢ The ability to love will bloom in your heart and you will see the world through the eyes of Love.

Mother Mary - This love will spread out to those around you and you will be a positive influence on everyone you meet. You will in fact raise the consciousness of those whom you interact with.

Millian ⌢ When we say you will change, we mean your heart will be more loving and kind. You will understand the joy of Enlightenment and the feeling of being connected in the great Oneness of the Universe.

Quan Yin ⌢ We also mean that your attitude towards life will change.

Aurelia ⌢Do not be afraid of change. These are changes for good that will make you a better person—more kind and loving. Your life will be enriched.

Sheylana - We are going to speak today about why you must ask for the *Rites of Initiation*.

Saint Germain ⌢ The *Rites of Initiation* are required to begin your Path toward Ascension. You must be able to clear all karmic debt and you must intend to stay on your path.

Lord Sananda ⌢ Your decision should not be taken lightly because it will change your life.

Lady Nada ⌢ Your life will change in every way that is good and positive, but you may lose friends or family members who do not recognize the path you are on.

Sheylana ⌒ You are not to worry about when Ascension will take place—instead, focus on where you are on your Path.

Aurelia ⌒ Do not think that just because you ask for the *Rites of Initiation* that your work is done. You must also begin to view your whole life differently.

Rites of Initiation

Anahamar ⌒ These Rites can only be given by the Ascended Masters of Telos. Do not worry about the reasons for this. Just believe. Many who belong to the world's religions will have difficulty accepting our words: of this we understand. Know that God has given his blessing to this process.

Lady Nada ⌒ We are now instructing many people at night while they sleep. It can be done this way so as not to interrupt your daily life.

Lord Sananda ⌒ We will now talk about why these lessons are necessary. Your many [re]incarnations have accumulated much karma. You most atone for the karma from all your past lives if you wish to ascend.

Lord Millian ⌒ We also want you to know that you don't have to worry. This can all be accomplished very easily while you sleep. You will feel refreshed and so much lighter when the weight of all this karma has been lifted from your soul.

Adama ⌒ We will speak now of your lessons at night. When you go to sleep, set your intention to come to Telos and your Guides will take you there.

Quan Yin ⌒ We will then take you to the various temples where you will learn how to clear all your karma from past lives.

Aurelia ⌒ I am Aurelia. Karma is something that you [can] accrue from wrong doing in this and past lives. And by "wrong doing" I mean anything that is not loving and kind.

Hilarion ⌒ At each Temple different lessons are learned and different karmic debts are released. Afterwards you will feel so refreshed and lightened.

Mother Mary ⌒ We wish you to know that this releasing of karma is what breaks your need for reincarnation. You cleanse your past and start anew.

> **"The** *Rites of Initiation* **can be given to any one, no matter what their [Earth] age."** —ADAMA

Adama ⌒ We will talk about how even the youngest child may prepare. The *Rites of Initiation* can be given to any one, no matter what their age. I know you will ask, "But how does a child know to ask for the Rites?" They can ask when their Angel (or Guide) takes them at night to the Temples. In their etheric body they are no longer limited by age and can ask for the Rites at that time.

Mother Mary ⌒ We of Telos wish to tell you that every effort is made to ensure as many are given the opportunity to ask for the *Rites of Initiation* as possible.

Body Changes

Adama ⌒ We will talk on the need to prepare your body for the Ascension Process. I want you to know that the cosmic forces coming to Earth will affect all life, even the plants and animals. Those who have not prepared will die.

You have heard from Anahamar that the energies of the Universe will be affecting your bodies, but we need to discuss exactly what this means. Your bodies are made up of trillions of cells. These energies will affect the cellular structure in such a way that each cell will vibrate at a higher rate. This vibration will cause the cells to move.

When the cells move and drift further apart, you become less dense. Also, the vibration becomes high enough where you leave the 3rd dimension and enter a higher one.

The Ascension Process can only happen in people whose bodies have been prepared. This preparation includes both the physical and the spiritual.

Lord Lanto ⌒ The physical preparation includes being more crystalline. You do this by first starting to drink more water. Then eat more vegetables. Then you raise your bodies pH levels by choosing food that alkalize your system.

Lady Nada ⌒ Not only your physical body must change but your mind and spirit also as well.

Quan Yin ⌒ Your mind must reflect higher values and you must embrace the Light and Love of the creator.

Aurelia - This is not something to be undertaken lightly. It will change your life and you will not be the same—you will be much better.

Sheylana ⌒ We will talk about the need to prepare your body for the Ascension Process.

Adama ⌒ Because of the necessity to let in as much light as possible, your body must be transformed into a crystalline one. The cells will not be as they are now. This means that your very atoms will rearrange into a crystalline lattice, yet you will still be human and hardly notice the change.

Lord Sananda ⌒ Your body can only change if it is given the proper nutrition. This means more fruits and vegetables and less meat.

Quan Yin 〜 I want you to realize that what you eat becomes your body—so when you are going to sit down to your meal, pray over your food. Ask that it be made healthy for your body and sustain the highest level of vibration for your highest good.

Aurelia - You do not have to eat only vegetables. Some meat is all right but the more vegetables you eat, the better, because they alkalinize your system.

Lady Nada 〜 You do not have to be a vegetarian unless you wish to. When I say you don't have to be a vegetarian, I am not suggesting that eating meat is the best thing for your body. Many people would be turned away if we forced them to eat only vegetables. I believe that thanking the animal for sacrificing its life is always important and knowing how to end their life quickly and with as little pain as possible is the most powerful way of insuring disease-free food.

Sheylana 〜 We continue our talk about the need to prepare your bodies to ascend. It is very important that you do not consume the wrong types of food.

Adama 〜 What happens to your body is this: when you eat too much meat or drink too much caffeine, you shut off the energy centers in your cells. You actually decrease the mitochondrial activity and your cells become sluggish. They do not want to renew themselves nor do they function at their top capacity.

Lord Sananda 〜 It is very important for you to realize that what you eat is as important as what you think.

Lady Nada 〜 Your bodies are like wonderful machines but they need the proper fuel to run.

Sheylana 〜 I want to mention that not only should one eat better, but exercise also. This can be as simple as walking more or taking time to stretch in the morning; it wakes the body's cells and helps the energy flow. *

CHAPTER SEVEN

The Sacred Temples

Sheylana ⌒ I will speak about the reason for your learning at the various Temples. Each night you will go in your etheric body to the various Temples to learn and be instructed by an Ascended Master. This continues until you pass each Initiation. Finally, you go to the Temple of Ascension and your name is recorded.

Lord Lanto ⌒ We also wish to tell you that each Temple will help you heal your past lives as well as this one.

Millian ⌒ We will speak about going to the *Temple of Immortality*. This is where you come after your physical body dies and your Soul leaves to return home. At the Temple you go through a Life Review and contemplate whether you met the objectives and goals you wished to accomplish in the life you just left. Not only do you review your life, but the Ascended Masters help you as well.

At this time you decide if you want to reincarnate again or continue to learn in other ways. You are given choices as to how you can learn to grow. Many choose to reincarnate again because it's the faster way to learn, but others will take time between lives to aid others by being Guides or helping out in the Temples or attending classes. There is so much that awaits you on the other side and we do not sit around on clouds all day.

Paul the Venetian ⁓ You are given lessons in life to learn more when you come to the Temple at night. There you will receive instruction on not only love but forgiveness, because sometimes the greatest love involves being able to forgive someone who has hurt you.

Quan Yin ⁓ To forgive is to see the lesson in each incident and find a way to love.

Sheylana ⁓ We will speak on the subject of the Ascension Flame. You know that this flame exists in the Great Temple here in Telos but also in its sister city in Luxor, Egypt.

Adama ⁓ The power of the Ascension Flame is what will start the Ascension Process.

Lord Sananda ⁓ Not only will this sacred flame start the process but it will burn within the hearts of those who will be Ascending.

Lady Nada ⁓ You will feel the flame's power not only in your heart, but in the very essence of your being.

Quan Yin ⁓ I want you to know that this flame does not burn like the flame of your fire. Its flame is one of a heavenly sort and ignites the God Fire within you.

Aurelia ⁓ The Ascension Flame, in addition to the energies of space as the earth travels on her orbit, will both have their affects on your bodies. Only those who are prepared will be comfortable with this energy and use it to ascend.

Lord Matraiya ⁓ I have not spoken before, but now is a good time for me to tell you that at my Temple of Manifestation, you will need to be totally converted to a crystalline cell structure. I can only pass those who have done their preparation and have made the changes necessary to convert from a carbon-based cell structure to one of a crystalline form.

If you do not do this, you will not pass my Temple and you cannot proceed to the Great Hall of Ascension or have your name recorded by Lord Serapis Bey.

Lord Serapis Bey ∼ In my Temple of Ascension there is a log of all the Initiates who have passed all the tests of all the Temples. Unless your name is on this list you cannot ascend.

Archangel Metatron ∼ I will be the one who reads off the names on this list on the appointed day.

Adama ∼ I will answer the question of what to say to those who ask, "Why is Telos in charge of the Initiation Process?" We of Telos realize that many will have a problem with this. We do not pretend to be from any religion, nor do we favor any religion.

God is the one who granted us the great honor of making us Keepers of the Temple and we oversee the instructions of the Temples and we also determine when a person has learned enough to move on and continue their training in the next temple, until finally their name is recorded in the great Hall of Ascension.

Lady Nada ∼ *We of Telos also want you to know that karma can only be lifted at these Temples.* Even good works [deeds] done in this lifetime cannot remove karma from your past lives.

Sheylana ∼ We of Telos want to tell you that it is God's plan, not ours. He was the one who came to us and asked us to be the Keepers of the Temples, which we gladly did for these millions of years.

Quan Yin ∼ We of Telos have been watching over Mother Earth for millions of years and we are glad to be of service.

Aurelia ∼ The people of Telos are very happy to be teaching in the Temples and helping humanity. They have been waiting for this day for a long time. I can only encourage you to take advantage of this. ✳

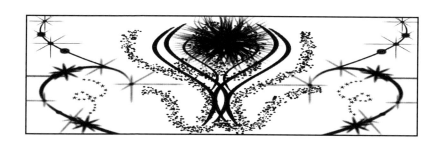

CHAPTER EIGHT

The Ascension

Aurelia ⌒ We are now ready to go into more detail on the Ascension Process.

Adama ⌒ It is my wish to tell you that the date for the Ascension of mankind will be on December 21, 2012. This date has been given to us by God himself.

Lord Sananda ⌒ You can believe this date is true because it is my word also. Our heavenly Father wishes people to know how much time they have left to prepare.

Lady Nada ⌒ I will also tell you to believe in this date and realize how little time is left and all that you must accomplish.

Ascended Masters ⌒ We also want to say that many will ascend before the December 21, 2012 date. The reason for this is to prepare the way for the great number of those who are to follow. Those who ascend early will have a chance to tell us what the others will need and what they will expect. All this will be done to make the transition as easy as possible.

Ascension is not just something that happens just once. There are many more dimensions above the fifth and many levels to each dimension, so your journey never really stops. A Soul must progress spiritually before going further. They can grow via many ways. We have temples where teaching continues and many attend classes and discussion groups. There are opportunities to serve others and grow by helping. You can meditate and pray. All these things help one grow spiritually. When a Soul feels ready, they can ask the teachers for advice and then pray to God. If God feels that they have progressed enough, they would be allowed to ascend to the next higher level.

With each Ascension, there is an increase in the vibration of the cells. The cells drift farther and farther apart, so the body becomes less and less dense. Eventually the cells are so far apart that [physical] form is lost entirely. We will say that this does not happen until the ninth-dimension and beyond. The time it takes a Soul to reach this level could be millions of years. There is nothing to fear in this process and no Soul is forced to ascend if they do not wish to or are not ready.

Humanity

Aurelia ◠ The Ascension Process is not going to hurt. In fact, quite the opposite: you will feel such joy and immense love that you will be in bliss.

Sheylana ◠ The human body is made up of millions of cells. When we ascend, those cells absorb light on a quantum level and begin to vibrate faster than is presently possible. This vibration causes a space to be created between the cells that grow larger and larger.

The bonds that have held the cells close together are broken and they drift apart. What happens to the body is not what you would expect. You do not explode or fly apart. What does happen is that the body changes from an organic form to one more crystal-line. Yes, this is possible. The process does not hurt—actually it is quite blissful.

Adama ◠ After your cells become filled with light energy and start to vibrate at a higher rate and move apart, you become less dense. Naturally this means that those who are not affected will no longer be able to see you.

Sheylana ⟶ What happens next is a miracle. Your vibrating cells transcend space and time to travel to either Earth2 or where ever you choose to go.

Lord Sananda ⟶ Many of you will want to know the science behind this transformation. On a quantum level the atoms in your cells embark on a journey through the black hole in your Sun and use it as a worm hole to another universe.

Adama ⟶ We of Telos wish to let you know that your auric field is a vital part of the Ascension Process. When the energy causes your cells to drift apart, it is the auric field that keeps them from going too far. It is your safety net. When you are drawn through the black hole it is the auric field that protects you from gamma and other radiation. After the 9th dimension you no longer need an auric field.

Adama ⟶ Your Sun has been shining on humanity for millions of years but not always with the same intensity.

Lord Sananda ⟶ It is correct that the number of humans would affect the Sun's intensity.

Quan Yin ⟶ The energy from humanities energy field is not radioactive, but once it enters space it can change and does. It becomes gamma radiation particles and others that are more able to exist in space. The Sun is not affected by the black hole because it is not really a star.

Aurelia ⟶ The Sun is really not in your dimension. You are its true energy. It reflects your light. It can only be seen as it truly is by beings of a higher vibration. Yes, there is a black hole near its center. The Sun does not get pulled in because the black hole is in your dimension and the Sun is in another.

When A Sun Is Not A Star

Sheylana ⌒ I will comment on the black hole in the Sun. Yes, there is a black hole present there! You do not see it because your eyes are not looking at the real energy of the Sun or its surroundings. What you see in your daily lives is the reflection of energy from all the people. It is more than theory. The Sun and its solar flares are not what you think they are.

Adama ⌒ Your Sun is actually a giant solar mirror in that it reflects the energy of your auras. This reflection has been going on since before recorded history. On a quantum level, your light travels from your auric field and goes out into space. Yes, your highest chakras indeed reach out into space. Now imagine that energy being caught, held and reflected back as the warmth of your Sun.

Aurelia ⌒ Your scientists actually know much of this but do not publish their theories for fear of public reaction. You are led to believe the Sun is a gaseous ball because if you knew its light was from your own energy, it would empower you.

Quan Yin ⌒ A solar flare is really an outlet for the energy of the people that is being collected. If that much energy were to be reflected back all at once it would destroy all biological life on Earth.

Sheylana ⌒ I believe that you see [the Sun as] a ball because it is your reality. Those in the 5th dimension see the Sun as a crescent shape consisting of an etheric material. *

Sheylana ⌇ When I tell you that the Sun in your sky is not a ball of gas but a big mirror, I am talking on very simple terms. On a quantum level, the Sun is made up of etheric atoms that vibrate on a frequency that is not third-dimensional.

Lady Nada ⌇ You see a ball of gas because that is what you have been told it is and so your mind takes the easy way out and sees what it is told.

Quan Yin — If you looked at the Sun through a telescope with special filters, so as not to hurt your eyes, you would see a flat surface.

Lord Sananda ⌇ We will speak now about how you are going to know when to ascend.

Archangel Metatron ⌇ It will be my job to signal all Souls to begin the Ascension Process. You will feel my call in the core of your being and your cells will respond by increasing their vibration. This will happen as a massive group. All those who have prepared will begin the Ascension Process. This process will not take long. We are talking a matter of a few minutes. The Light from so many souls Ascending will be seen clear into space—where many of your Star Brothers and Sisters[*] await you.

Aurelia ⌇ No, you do not die. Your body will be the one you are familiar with, but you can improve it by making it younger and more fit. You can also be taller or more slender, if you wish.

Sheylana ⌇ We will speak more on the Ascension Flame, what it does to your bodies and when it will activate. Your bodies are becoming more crystalline and holding more light. They can radiate light and love. You will find this happening when you think happy, joyful thoughts. The Ascension Flame will magnify this affect one thousand times and you will become beacons of love shinning for all the universe to see.

....
[*]   For more information on this subject, read *2012 - **Mother Earth Wants You!*** by Marc and Gail Ries.

Adama ⌒ When the Ascension Flame is activated within your heart its Light will raise your vibration to a higher level, one which your present dimension can not hold.

Lord Sananda ⌒ This means that you will ascend to a higher dimension of existence.

Lady Nada ⌒ This process takes only minutes and it does not hurt. In fact, it feels wonderful.

Mother Mary ⌒ Yes, I have undergone this process and you take your physical body with you to the higher dimension, but it will be a better body—renewed, younger and more beautiful because of it's light and love.

"[A]s your cells vibrate faster and begin to move apart, you will experience bliss. The reason for this is the energy involved is so closely related to the God Energy that for the first time since you incarnated, your Soul remembers the feeling of being back home." —*SHEYLANA*

Sheylana ⌒ I will go into why you will have so many special feelings. By this I mean that as your cells vibrate faster and begin to move apart, you will experience bliss. The reason for this is the energy involved is so closely related to the God Energy that for the first time since you incarnated, your Soul remembers the feeling of being back home.

It will be the most blissful experience of your life. There is no pain involved. Your cells will drink up the energy and vibrate with such love and power that your whole body will rejoice.

Ascended Masters ⌒ We have told you how the energy will excite the molecules of your body to vibrate and move farther apart. Next we will describe what happens after this state is reached.

Once your molecules drift apart they are then raised into the next dimension. This continues until they are raised high enough and can sustain the vibration of the 5th dimension. At this point you have disappeared to those remaining on Earth, although you can still see them.

Next your molecules will move up toward the Sun and through the black hole which is at its center. You will not be destroyed, nor will you disintegrate, because this is no ordinary black hole but a worm hole to the Vega Galaxy. You will have memory of this journey and you will be able to see all the fantastic sights along the way. You will be able to communicate with your fellow Souls who are [also] Ascending and you will be so happy.

Lord Sananda ⌒ I too think you will love the experience and you will be able to watch as the Earth also ascends.

Aurelia ⌒ You will have many questions I am sure. Let me say that this process is one approved by God.

Sheylana ⌒ The Archangel Metatron will read names from [the list in the *Temple of Ascension* of all those who have passed the *Rites of Initiation*] on the final day when the Mass Ascension is to take place. At his signal all will begin the Ascension Process. The reason for this is so that humanity will sound a clear tone as they all ascend. *This tone will be noted by the Pleiadians who will use the information to correct their own genetic code in the future—and save their race.*

Adama ⌒ The Mass Ascension of humanity will not only help the Pleiadians, but also other universes as well.

Archangel Gabriel ⌒ I want to tell you that Archangel Metatron will signal the Great Ascension of Humanity by calling out to God and then releasing his Golden energy to all those whose names he has read. His energy will jump-start the Ascension Process in your cells, which will then use the cosmic energy coming to Earth at this time and the process will begin.

Aurelia ⌁ I know you have many questions. I can only say that for those who have prepared, this will be an amazing feeling. I can also say that this will not hurt if you have prepared. I must warn those who have not prepared that they will experience great discomfort as the cosmic forces come to Earth and many Souls will decide to pass from their lives at this time.

Lord Maitraya ⌁ It is my pleasure to tell you that all who ascend will be helped in the transition. There will be some getting used to in this new dimension and we will be here to help you adjust.

Aurelia ⌁ It is my pleasure to tell you of my experience. After making the transition from my earthly life, I was met by my family here in Telos. They were so supportive and loving. I had no fear or worries. It was a beautiful experience. I want you to know that your Ascension will be such a glorious experience and there will be such rejoicing in the heavens! All will be made ready for you and no one will be alone. We are awaiting your arrival and will be so happy on that day.

Mother Earth

Those who choose to not ascend in the "Mass Ascension" of 2012 still have a small opportunity of time to "Become". Mother Earth will continue on her journey towards Ascension, allowing others to ascend if they work hard.

It would appear that the most massive and destructive Earth Changes will occur after the year 2012 as Mother Earth goes through the process of removing her remaining karma. Somewhere around the year 2020 a shower of asteroids will hurtle toward earth and impact her surface with enough velocity to create vast craters and enough force to nudge her orbit closer to the "Sun".

The gravitational pull of the Sun will be such that Earth—now nudged out of her orbit by the asteroids—will be caught in its pull. It will cause enormous fluctuations in the poles and all manner of geomagnetic variations.

Eventually the earth will succumb to the pull and be drawn into the black hole in the middle of the Sun and be reincarnated in her fifth-dimensional form in the Vega Galaxy around the year 2029.

> **"Human life must either be ready for an energy shift or it must die; there will be no magic switch to a new reality or a different dimension for those not prepared."** —*LADY NADA*

As for the third-dimensional people of Earth still remaining after 2012, any that have survived the massive Earth Changes and the aftermath of multiple asteroid impacts will not survive Earth's journey through the black hole. In the interim, humans can still ask for and try to pass the *Rites of Ascension*.

↫

Lady Nada ↬ When the Earth approaches the Galactic Center, all life will be affected. Human life must either be ready for an energy shift or it must die; there will be no magic switch to a new reality or a different dimension for those not prepared.

Faconia (the Sirian) ↬ It is my pleasure to tell you we are in orbit around your planet and we are now watching you. As the Earth ascends we will pull our ship back to a safe distance, probably several hundred thousand miles past your planet (maybe more depending on the strength of the Sun's gravitational pull).

We wish to witness the Earth's final journey into the Sun, and then we will travel to the Vega Galaxy and watch her rebirth there. We will rejoice and give thanks to Prime Creator for this wonderful event.

You should tell the people of Earth that they are heroes. You will be tested by the powers that be and if they are able to Awaken, their reward will be grand indeed.

Gerenlus (the Sirian) ⌒ Your planet is so beautiful and about to ascend. It is an honor to witness such an event. You are going to either ascend with her or die. You have a choice to Awaken and join your Brothers and Sisters of the Stars or remain in the 3rd dimension. We hope you will choose to ascend and join us. The galaxies await your visits and the universes are looking forward to seeing you, so don't disappoint them.

The Universe

Ascended Masters ⌒ The Universe has many third-dimensional planets with life on them and many have developed space technologies beyond what you know. Many races are *of the Light*, but some are still *of the Dark*. I can say that when First Contact does occur, it will be with a the third-dimensional group from a Federation fleet.

> "WHEN HUMANITY ASCENDS IN MASS, IT WILL SEND A RIPPLE EFFECT NOT ONLY OUT FROM OUR PLANET IN OUR UNIVERSE, BUT IN PARALLEL UNIVERSES AS WELL. THIS RIPPLE EFFECT WILL ALSO TRAVEL THROUGH TIME INTO THE FUTURE." —*AURELIA*

The Ascension of Earth will affect many dimensions and universes. All of Creation will be helped by this loving planet that has waited so long to ascend. The benefits are so numerous. You will see it [the Earth's Ascension] happen as a newly Ascended being.

Ascension is not the end of this story. It is, however, a great beginning. You can not imagine all that you will do and see. The Universe is large and we are able to travel. I see you know of merkabas; we can manifest our own when needed or we can travel on a Federation ship. There are many that explore the different star systems and visit planets. We think most of the planets visited are fifth-dimensional.

When the earth ascends it will affect all universes and all the dimensions. The parallel universes will not merge but will be lifted up in vibration as well. As your Earth, ascends so will the Earth in other universes. There is a connection between you in parallel universes. If one ascends, you help the others by lifting their vibrations and making it easier for them to ascend.

Lord Sananda ∼ Different parallel universes will experience a raising of their vibration, all because of humanity's achievement.

Lady Nada ∼ You are going to be surprised at all the effects your Mass Ascension will produce, not only for this Universe, but others as well.

"I AM THE CAPTAIN OF A FEDERATION STARSHIP. THE PURPOSE OF THE FEDERATION [OF PLANETS] IS TO FOSTER BROTHERHOOD AND FELLOWSHIP AMONG MANY STAR RACES. MEMBERSHIP IN THE FEDERATION IS OPEN TO ALL ENLIGHTENED RACES WHO ARE *OF THE LIGHT* AND KNOW THE WAYS OF LOVE AND THE PRIME CREATOR, INCLUDING ASCENDED HUMANS." —GRENADIAN, AN ARCTURIAN[11]

Quan Yin ∼ Have no doubt that this is all part of God's plan.

Aurelia ∼ When humanity ascends in mass, it will send a ripple effect not only out from our planet in our Universe, but in parallel universes as well. This ripple effect will also travel through time into the future. It will be an event unlike any so far in recorded time. ✳

"YOU MUST BE THE CHANGE YOU WISH TO SEE IN THE WORLD." —MAHATMA GANDHI, INDIAN LEADER

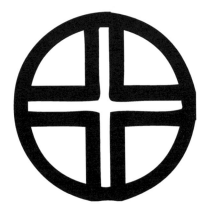

CHAPTER NINE

Where Are We Headed?

Quan Yin ⌣ You are truly blessed to have this opportunity to learn and grow. God has given humanity a great dispensation at this time because never before in the history of mankind have so many been given the opportunity to ascend at one time. Use this gift wisely and believe.

Sheylana ⌣ The Ascension Process is only half the story. There is also what happens after you ascend. You will have some choices to make and you will find that they are all wonderful.

Adama ⌣ I personally will greet you when you ascend and will welcome you home. Do not be afraid, we will have everything you need and you will be taken care of. Your family and friends will be here too, those you do not even remember as of yet and those who have gone before you. It will be a day of such rejoicing.

Lady Nada ⌣ You will be a being in a higher dimension and the physical laws of your present dimension will no longer apply. You will have a new set of Cosmic Laws that will apply and you will know these laws because they are part of your Soul.

Adama ⌣ Once you ascend you will have much to do. There are always groups meeting to talk, grow and learn. There are teachers of hobbies and crafts. There are musicians and people laughing and children playing. It is so wonderful and there is always time to enjoy family and friends. You are never rushed and there are no watches because time as you know it does not exist.

Millian ⌒ I want to say that we of Telos look forward to seeing many of our family return to us.

Lady Nada ⌒ I also want to say that you will be welcomed with open arms and much joy, for your coming home is cause for much celebration and all will be made ready for you.

Ascended Masters ⌒ After Ascension, you will come to Earth2 for your transition because you will need help adjusting [to the 5th dimension]. Once you are comfortable with your new life, you can then choose where you would like to go.

The Ascended Masters will be teaching many classes on various subjects to prepare you for making the best possible decision. I want you to know that Ascension is not the end of your Path, just the beginning.

"WE NEVER INTRUDE ON ANOTHER... WE NEVER INVITE OURSELVES INTO A GROUP WITHOUT ASKING IF IT IS ALRIGHT TO JOIN... WE ALSO SHARE FREELY WHAT WE CREATE OR MAKE WITH OUR HANDS." —ASCENDED MASTERS

There is much exchange and we love to learn about other worlds. Learning is very valued, but so is fun and relaxation. There is time to be with family and friends. For those who like doing so, we have crafts and hobbies of all sorts. There is music and laughter. We also believe that anyone who wants to learn something [new] will be given every opportunity to do so. We have many teachers who love helping others learn. This is as long or short as you need it to be.

We know this is not easy for you to understand, but you will be able to comprehend when you get here.

We think you will enjoy leaving your watches and clocks behind. You will never be late or early again and there will always be enough time for any project you wish to do.

We also want to go over some of the rules we live by. Life in the 5th dimension is very good and easy, but to remain so, we must respect each other. We never intrude on another. We always ask their permission before contacting them telepathically. By "permission," we mean we inquire if it is a good time to talk. We never invite ourselves into a group without asking if it is alright to join. I think these are basic rules of politeness. We also share freely what we create or make with our hands.

Earth2

Lord Sananda ⌒ I will tell you that among your choices is going to Earth2—a planet created just for those who ascend and are fifth-dimensional. I do know that you may have family or friends who will not ascend. You may visit them but they will not have bodies as yours will be.

Ascended Masters ⌒ When you arrive in the Vega Galaxy there will be a planet especially prepared for you. It is a planet many times bigger than your present Earth. It is very beautiful and has no pollution or things you presently have on your world. This Earth2, as we call it, will be inhabited by many races and all the Kingdoms. All will live in peace and harmony. Archangel Gabriel has [already] spoken about all the wonders you will encounter on Earth2, so we won't go into them here. If you want to learn more, we recommend listening to the Benu Too CD on Earth2*.

Once you arrive there will be a period of adjustment. Not only will you get to decide how you want to look, but how you are going to spend your time. You will arrive with nothing, not even

* ***EARTH 2 AND YOU***, Karen Cook, Benu Too Inc., Albuquerque, NM.

clothes, but have no concerns. You will be met with love and all will be provided. This time of adjustment is when you will learn to manifest your clothes and food, if you desire to eat. You will have the opportunity to visit friends and family. You can attend classes or discussions on every subject you can think of.

We can say that we have many races that will be living on Earth2. If you like meeting new beings, you will enjoy being there; not only Star Brothers and Sisters live there, but members of the Other Kingdoms. We think meeting a unicorn or a dragon will be an exciting experience for many. Also, learning that flowers can talk and can be very sassy will make many people laugh. There is much laughter in the higher dimensions.

There is no need of money or even of a barter system. We think many on Earth2 will enjoy the freedom from worrying about money. You can manifest homes, clothes, food and you can also grow food and make clothes—it is your choice.

We believe that we have to respect all life, so our homes are not made of wood, but of a manifested glass block design. The homes do not have to be large, even though at first some may desire that, because you can change the design as your needs require. You can add a large room if you want to entertain or you can add a bedroom if you want to rest. Your home can change to suit your requirements by merely thinking about changing it. We laugh at the surprise this causes.

We are free from worry about money, jobs, housing—even child upbringing. There is no need for nannies or baby sitters. Our children are raised in a community of love. If the parents need a break, someone is always there to look out and care for the young ones; we value our young and cherish all life. We see only happiness on the faces of both the children and the adults here. We think of this as heaven because we are closer to God and there is much joy and happiness.

We have the ability to access Universal Knowledge and know many things which you can only imagine. Even with such knowledge, there is still room for new thoughts. We love helping other beings and planets and God's Universe is ever expanding and new life coming into being. There is always something new to think about.

We have much to tell you about Earth2. You will be so happy there. Time will no longer exist as you now know it. You will be free to take as long as needed, whether it's visiting friends or family or having wonderful discussions or working on an art project. Imagine always having enough time and never being late. In the 5th dimension there is still a progression of time but it is not the same as you [now] experience. There is no sunrise or sunset, unless you want to see one.

The planet does not have to act as in your [current] dimension. The Cosmic Laws of the 5th dimension are different from the third. Duality does mask many truths and what you presently consider the Laws of Science are not necessarily true in higher dimensions.

> **"In higher dimensions souls are interviewed and both the couple and the child to be must agree and feel comfortable with each other before conception takes place."** —ASCENDED MASTERS

We have much to say about families on Earth2. We have many children who are loved and cherished. No child is unwanted, nor do we have teen pregnancy. Children come to couples who are prepared for the experience. It is not something taken lightly. Only loving couples who, after deciding they want a child and after long preparation and reflection, go ahead and conceive. Nor is the process the same as you now know.

In higher dimensions Souls are interviewed and both the couple and the child to be must agree and feel comfortable with each other before conception takes place. The pregnancy also does not last your usual nine months; instead it lasts only a matter of weeks. The birth is much easier because there is no fear around it; the mother is showered with love and energy and the infant welcomed by so much positive energy that it glows.

Here, children grow quickly. Growth happens on a spiritual level, rather than a physical one. What this means is that as the child grows in spirituality, their physical body matures. They are guided along their spiritual path by all, so raising a child is a community thing and there is no burden on the parents. The parents can spend as much time as they want with the child because they have all the time they need. There are no time schedules, no jobs that they must run off to and no bills to pay. In higher dimensions everything is provided. There is no want and no desire that cannot be fulfilled.

In higher dimensions we still enjoy recreation. Music, song, dance, hand-crafted items are all very much valued. We love working with our hands; even though we can manifest, we enjoy the art of doing.

Those who enjoy gardening will love the higher dimensions because they can communicate with their plants. We have flowers that are beyond human words to describe.

Sheylana ⌇ People on Earth2 will have the choice to become Spirit Guides to non-Ascended humans who decide to remain in the lower vibrations and reincarnate on third-dimensional planets.

Ascended Earth

After Mother Earth ascends, Souls may decide to reincarnate there as fifth-dimensional *adults*, since there are no pre-existing "parents" as such. They will find this new Earth much changed. The Ascended Earth [Earth1] will be a paradise—lush, green, and pollution free. Starting out, there will be no buildings, cars, or other man made things. Humans will be able to create what they need to survive including homes built of self-manifested glass-like blocks.

These newly incarnated Souls will be given the chance to start anew and live in peace. They will have greater knowledge of themselves as Divine Beings who are part of the Cosmic Oneness— they will know that the trees and animals, and the planet they now reside on are sentient beings deserving respect as Brothers and Sisters from the Other Kingdoms.

Archangel Gabriel also tells us that there will be reincarnation cycles on Earth1—one of those "exception to the rules" situations. Those who incarnate on Ascended Earth for the first time will be in the lowest vibrational level of the 5th dimension. As they grow spiritually and increase their vibration levels, they will be given the chance to ascend. Those who "Mass Ascended" from Mother Earth will have Ascended to a high enough vibrational level that reincarnation is no longer necessary.

⌒

Sheylana ⌒ The people who reincarnate on Ascended Earth [Earth1] will be fifth-dimensional and will be people who lead good lives but did not complete or get the *Rites of Initiation* for Ascension. They will no longer have Duality but will need Guides to help them make better choices and help them grow spiritually. Their [Spirit] Guides will come from higher dimensions.

Other Opportunities

Lady Nada ⌒ Your other choices will be to go to a new Universe [the "Golden" Universe] created by Archangel Michael. It will have many planets and there will be many to choose from.

Ascended Masters ⌒ We will cover more on the subject of what happens after you ascend. You already know how your body will ascend and where it will go, but you do have some choices. At first you will arrive on Earth2 and be met by family and friends. You will have time for making the transition to 5th dimension life in this new timelessness. Once you have acclimated yourself and feel comfortable, your real choices begin. You can stay on Earth2, you can become a Guide for the people on Ascended Earth or you can go to the Golden Universe.

We see you are thinking of the Golden Universe and yes, it is fifth-dimensional.

The Golden Universe was created by Archangel Michael. Yes, Archangels have the power to create worlds. This Universe is full of many wonderful planets, each unique in its own way. The opportunity here is to start a new world of your own and build a society that is fresh and has no Duality. You can begin with no karmic debt and live as God always intended. This is a great gift.

Those who do not ascend and still reincarnate in lower vibrations do not have Duality but still require help in making choices that will lift them up into higher vibrations, so that is why they have Guides. Your choices after Ascension do include being Guides and yes, only humans need [Spirit] Guides.

We believe that if a Soul wished to travel, they could ask for a position aboard a [Galactic] Federation [of Light] Starship. You have many Souls on board ships now who were once human and they have reincarnated as Star Brothers and Sisters because they wanted to travel the Universe. They [first] reincarnated as a third-dimensional alien.

A Soul who dies and does not ascend can only reincarnate as third-dimensional, therefore they could not be on a Federation ship of the 5th dimension. ✳

The Five Secret Rays

Lord Sananda ⌒ The Seven Rays and the five "secret" Rays are now [January 2010] being activated within all those who have gone through various Temples and have passed all the *Rites of Initiation*.

I believe that each person will experience the activation differently. Each person's abilities will be different: some may see "energy," others will hear tones or feel vibrations.

These things signify that the secret rays are coming on-line. Do not worry [if you are not experiencing them yet]: these rays are often subtle and will become apparent over time.

"BELIEVE"

CHAPTER TEN

Questions and Answers

Why should I believe what the author is writing?

It is not the authors' responsibility to make you believe what is written within. If the information does not resonate with the reader (feel right) then you may not spiritually be in the place where you can believe it as Truthful and may be choosing to take a different route to Enlightenment, both in this life and in the hereafter.

Even if you chose not to believe now, the mere act of reading this book may lead to synchronistic events that shape your life and give you additional chances to accept—or reject—the information within. The books and CDs listed in the Reference Section may be good starting points.

By the end of the current Ascension Process cycle it will be possible to say that everyone had at some time been given the opportunity to take a new Path out of reincarnation, Duality and the Veil. This book is but one mechanism God has provided for giving you (the reader) the opportunity to re-orientate your life towards the Path that leads to the Ascension Process. Each of us can choose however, via free will, not to achieve the lessons and opportunities their Soul wanted to learn and experience in this incarnation.

The authors are not creating the mechanism for how Ascension will happen in our lifetimes—we are only passing on the information as channeled by those *of the Light* serving God in the higher dimensions and "decreed by God".

I believed that Lightworkers would 'ascend' in frequency on this planet and in Light and wisdom assist those that were not Awake, while still living on this planet?

When you are living in the Light and using your Light and Wisdom to assist others, *if they ask for assistance*, in becoming Awakened then you are raising your frequency while still living on this planet. As an Ascended being, this book has mentioned but a few of the many opportunities to look forward to in assisting those "not Awake". They just won't be on our 3D planet Earth.

Ascension itself is the act of moving one's physical body into a higher dimension/vibration (your Soul/Higher Self is already there); Ascension will be in a physical body that has changed its body cells and density to make it suitable for life in the higher dimensions.

Please remember that God has said he has "granted" Mother Earth's request to ascend during *this* particular multi-million-year cycle through our Universe, having missed several past opportunities to do so. God has *only* given humanity "special dispensation" for an *opportunity* to ascend.

If Mother Earth were *not* Ascending, then those humans that did ascend could essentially just become residents of 5D Telos, if they wished. But Earth *is* Ascending. In fact, Telos has been (will be) recreated on Earth2.

This material makes me fearful and I am trying to make some sense of this. Why do I feel this way?

If you told a child this information, before they were "influenced" by their parents, their environment, religion, government, media, technology and peer-pressure, they would probably just say, "OK. I'll go outside and play until then." Children tend to live in the Now and accept whatever the world is offering. Older folks may feel fear because all of these outside influences, along with Duality and the Veil, have helped keep the Truth hidden and when we do see bits and pieces of the Truth, it forces us to rethink and re-evaluate all aspects of our currently-held spiritual and physical beliefs.

We can also feel fear and negativity because we have allowed our Ego, in self-preservation mode, to filter our thoughts, beliefs and experiences before they reach our heart instead of the other way around. Judgments made by the Ego, whether of a positive *or* negative nature, creates an energetic structure of limitation.

One useful method to help keep our egos in perspective is by being in the "Now", which is why teachers of the Now (e.g. Eckhart Tolle) have been embraced by many on the Path. By allowing your Heart to formulate beliefs, rather than the Ego, you can be surrounded by all of the possibilities of Divine Creation at all times.

For those family and friends who do not Awaken before Mass Ascension, am I just supposed to leave them here and let them fend for themselves?

Ultimately, we are only truly responsible for ourselves. All others, including family, friends and non-friends, are here on their own journeys, even though through Duality and the Veil we have accepted a communal "world" through our co-creation. No human can know exactly why the person next to them, be they family or friend, reincarnated on Earth at this time and what they wished to accomplish spiritually doing it. Which also implies that we, as individuals, do not know who will—or won't—ascend.

What if your family and friends ascend and you do not because you assumed they would not? It is very likely that "fending on their own" was one of the lessons they wished to experience if they chose not to ascend and that by our influence, and their free will to choose alternatives, we are depriving them of the experience they had incarnated for.

What is the point of trying to move forward in our current lives, to make repairs to one's home, pay our bills, go to school, work, and etcetera?

If you truly believe that you are alive on Earth now so you can buy a house, repair the house, pay bills and taxes on that house, go to work, etc. then no one is saying, "Don't do that." If that is what you wish to do, even after death, you could choose to reincarnate in a similar, or possibly less advanced third-dimensional environment and planet.

On the other hand, if you believe that you are on Earth to try and find out that houses, debt slavery, taxes, paying for and participating in wars, working for someone else's agenda, attending religious and governmental schools that teach what those in power want you to learn instead of the Truth, etc. are essentially not important for your Soul's progression on its spiritual Path then look around; there are plenty of opportunities to learn those lessons and know that all that will cease to exist when you pass from this third-dimensional body. These non-spiritual aspects of the 3rd dimension will not then have the power to create your spiritual Path.

If we already know that there is an end date why bother doing anything? Why don't we all sit under a tree and vegetate?

We don't know for sure, but would guess that many humans—including Jesus and Buddha—had some very enlightening moments come to them while sitting under a tree and "vegetating."

Life has been "brutal" for quite a while. We doubt that those who have died, in the Spanish Inquisition for example, felt that life at that time was a piece-of-cake. Rather than repeat those lives of brutality, God is essentially giving each human the option, for we each have free will, to choose to end this third-dimensional lifestyle and reap the benefits of Ascension.

There are still things to do if you wish to ascend—this book has tried to point out those basic things that need to happen on a physical and spiritual level; be kind and loving and live each day without imposing negativity on other beings (in all the Kingdoms), assist your body in becoming a better vessel for Ascension through nutrition and lifestyle, asking for the *Rites of Ascension* (which involves passing through all of the Sacred Temples to remove karma), surviving the Time of Darkness, dealing with the incursion of negative extraterrestrials and staying alive long enough so you can be around for the Ascension Process itself.

It is necessary to be alive to be able to ascend. Either through spiritual development (being able to communicate with your Guides or Guardians or members of the Other Kingdoms), insight or intuition, you need to not find yourself in the wrong place at the wrong time.

Will you find yourself detached enough from your physical possessions that you could quickly leave your house and home if you felt "intuitively" an earthquake or tidal wave were coming soon? Or would you choose to say and possibly die with your earthly possessions? Would you choose to stay and potentially die if a "loved one" chose not to leave in the same situation? Or would you be Awakened enough to grasp that we are all on our own journeys, and for that reason, the right to chose one's Path—being it to "stay" or "leave"—is one of the most unique gifts God has given us?

The thought of a fifth-dimensional body does not seem that important when thinking about what I will be leaving behind and there is even more work to do beyond Ascension. This is supposed to make me happy?

What meaning would your life have if there was not some goal you were working towards? Your existence is not some freak biological accident, but one of a careful cosmic design intended to give you every opportunity to move off the wheel of reincarnation that was set in motion eons ago.

If the environment and trappings of this third-dimensional life make you "jump for joy" then you can still pursue them in this life and whatever form of existence you decide to pursue after you pass from this life. Nothing has changed. Before you read this book there were no guarantees that over the next few years you, or a loved one near you, might die from war, disease, Earth Changes, crime or accident (if you believe in accidents). This can still happen if you allow it to happen, either by action or non-action.

Do you really wish to stagnate? If God had chosen not to experience growth, would our Universe even exist? Do you really want to "sit on a cloud and play the harp" for all eternity? It has been channeled to us that one of the reasons why Duality and the Veil came into existence is that the Demigods essentially got **bored**! It has also been told to us that essentially the **only** thing you can count on is change; change is the nature of the cosmos. Whether you ascend in this lifetime or not, there is always "even more work to do" no matter what dimension you are in.

How can I go forward in this life knowing that each day is that much closer to my demise on this planet, my leaving my family?

The point is that Ascension offers you a way to leave the current Earth with your physical body, without the trauma of what we humans call "death" and with all the benefits that "living" in the fifth dimension has to offer.

Before you read this book you already knew that each day you lived was a day closer to your "demise." You also had no idea when you would be leaving this planet nor did you know if you would be leaving before or after your other family members left. If you choose to not ascend this still holds true. You still have the free will and the choices available that could "accidently" end your life by tomorrow, next week or next year. You still have to be alive to be able to ascend. There will also be some humans who will ascend before the Mass Ascension and after, including those Ascending from their incarnation on Earth1 (the Ascended Earth).

The Ascended Masters and other beings of Light have repeatedly said that our third-dimensional minds can never fully grasp the implications and operations of the higher dimensions, which is why belief, faith and trust are powerful tools in our current dimension. Once you have left the third dimension, you will no longer be limited by a 3D brain and will realize we are all part of the One and can never truly be separated (unless we choose to be).

**"THERE IS NO DEATH,
BUT THERE IS A BELIEF IN DEATH."
—FROM "A COURSE IN MIRACLES"**[12]

The following is one example of which we speak, as it has been said by Archangel Gabriel that most Earthlings on the Ascension Path have had many thousands of past incarnations, both as humans, as non-humans on Earth and as Extraterrestrial beings, both humanoid and otherwise. Let's say that you had a grandfather that you loved, who died as an old gentleman some 40 years ago. During that time, the Soul you knew as "Grandpa" reincarnated back to Earth, and ultimately died as a teenager and is now back in the realm of the In Between. After you ascend, how will you know what this Soul "looks" like? Is this Soul the young man who died, the old man who was your "Grandpa" or one of the many thousands of forms this Soul has taken on since starting on the wheel of reincarnation?

The truth is that as a higher-dimensional being, you will intuitively know who this Soul is from their energy vibration and you can choose to envelope their energy with whatever visual manifestation you feel most comfortable with. Also know that some of the people who have given you the most "grief" on Earth are probably the Souls you love the most on the other side, since they would be the ones, out of the love they have for you, willing to do the "dirty work", so to speak, in creating those difficult situations you envisioned you needed to learn the spiritual lessons you wished to learn on Earth during this incarnation.

When you ascend, you will be able to greet not only those you knew in your last incarnation on Earth, but those you knew from any past incarnation on Earth. You will be able to greet those that pass over. You can help them transition and adjust and if they chose to incarnate again, you might even decide to be their Guardian Angel or Spirit Guide, if you wanted to continue to help them. Just realize, however, that Souls who pass over rather than ascend have fewer choices available to them, including how they can interact with the "physical" world of Ascended beings (which is why you would need to ascend to join the Galactic Federation, for example).

Until I read this book, I was truly looking forward to my Ascension, thinking that I would simply be lighter, more in tune with the higher dimensions and helping others to Awaken. Help me to grasp the wonder and delight in this upcoming event.

You will be lighter, you will be in tune with the higher dimensions and you can choose to help others in the lower dimensions to Awaken. You will not age, be sick, need to make money or have to worry about finding food, transportation or a place to live. You will be Enlightened, Awakened and have access to Universal Knowledge. You will not be under the constraints of linear time; you will never be late and you have all the time you need. You will not be forced to do anything you do not wish to do.

What is not delightful and wonderful about that?

Ascension is the process that will bring an end to your need to continue in the cycles of Duality and reincarnation and the Veil. What is special about this time is that the whole of Humanity has been given that choice. Ascension allows you to retain those parts of your current human personality that are compatible with the higher dimension you are moving to—a dimension that is closer to God (and God is Love).

Moving to the higher dimensions gives you the opportunity to not pay taxes or bills (there is no need for money), to attend classes of many kinds (or just access the Library of Universal Knowledge), to recreate your body, your clothes, your living space as you wish (whenever you wish). You can also relax or visit with friends and family for as long as you like—no one is forced to do anything they do not wish to do.

Ascension gives you the opportunity to become Guides for those that have decided to continue their spiritual lessons in the 3rd dimension, to work towards becoming an Angel, or to work or teach in the Sacred Temples. Ascension gives you the opportunity to become part of the real Star Trek™ adventure, by signing up with the Galactic Federation and journeying through the cosmos in one of their Light ships.

This book IS supposed to help you grasp the "wonder and delight in this upcoming event." What this book cannot do, however, is change you or your beliefs. Only you can do that. Not everyone (every Soul) is on the same Path or at the same spot on that Path. Not every Soul will ascend in this cycle. Not every Soul wishes to ascend during this cycle. This is not good versus bad or right vs. wrong. As Archangel Gabriel would probably say, "Where ever you are now is where you are supposed to be."

One thing that will happen if you do not ascend is that you will have no physical form and you will not be able to interact in a physical way as we do here on Earth. The only way to ascend at a future time, barring Divine Intervention, is by reincarnating again into a physical form from which you can ascend. However, when reincarnating, you would not be the same being you are now, because much of our physical and personality characteristics are a product of our birth environment and life experiences.

"AM I THEREFORE BECOME YOUR ENEMY, BECAUSE I TELL YOU THE TRUTH?"
—*PAUL THE APOSTLE TO THE GALAIANS (GALATIANS 4:16)*

This book is just what it is—words printed on paper. They have no power *unless* you give them that power. ✳

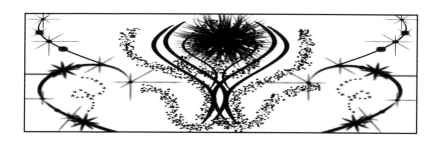

CHAPTER ELEVEN

Conclusion

The time of great change is upon us. This change has been called many names: Rapture, the Great Shift, the Golden Age, etc. We have called it *The Ascension Process*. The purpose of this book is to give you information to think about, a starting point for "Becoming" and a method to invoke the *Rites of Initiation*.

We hope that many, especially those reading this book, have progressed spiritually enough to know what has the ring of Truth to it. Because of free will and the Law of Attraction, the Dark are also allowed to put forward their own teachers, authors and information. These are but one way to test your powers of understanding and discernment on the Path. A true Teacher *of the Light* will never force upon you any teachings that you can not understand or find intuitively unacceptable.

You can either accept or reject the realty of Ascension because *the decision is now and always has been totally yours*: "For many are called, but few are chosen." Those who accept the call and prepare will have more choices open to them. If you need help, you only have to ask your Spirit Guides, Angels or the Ascended Masters—but allow the response to come in Divine Timing, rather than force it: you may, in this dimension at least, not know exactly what is best for you.

Every Soul and Path are unique. Those who do not resonate with the Truth will travel a longer Path to Ascension. If you cannot understand or accept the concepts put forward in this book, have no fear; you will evolve exactly at your own pace and one day you too will ascend. However, *not* accepting the reality of the coming Ascension does not mean your life will continue on in status-quo.

As Lady Nada has pointed out already, "Human life must either be ready for an energy shift or it must die; there will be no magic switch to a new reality... for those not prepared." You can not just wish to be part of this great shift and succeed; Ascension requires an effort on your part in raising your vibrations to be compatible with this coming energy shift.

Regardless of what many are predicting, the third-dimensional Earth we now call home will soon, relatively, no longer exist. We restate the point *that a loving God has heard <u>Mother Earth's prayers</u> for Ascension and has <u>granted her request</u>.* The **opportunity** for Mass Ascension is available to **us now** because Mother Earth **will** be Ascending. Which is why the Earth Changes have to happen as Mother Earth herself sheds karma and prepares for her own Ascension—not because God is an unloving entity or humanity has been less-than-ideal caretakers of their planet.

While *Earth does not need humanity in order to ascend* she is a kind and loving Soul and hopes, as do all the Kingdoms of Light, that as many humans as possible ascend before she does. God has granted humanity special dispensation at this time so we *might* ascend as well. God will allow all who Awaken to the *Truth* and *prepare spiritually* to ascend before Mother Earth does.

Mother Mary ⌢ My dear children, I have such love for you all!

Quan Yin ⌢ Know that we have taken compassion on you and revealed the Truth so you can take back the heritage of your Divine Power and be who God meant for you to be.

Sheylana ⌒ We of Telos have given you this news in the hope it speeds your desire to achieve the needed teaching and to complete the spiritual work you need to do in order to ascend.

Ascended Masters ⌒ We can say that all of your questions will be answered someday; however, right now it is beyond your understanding. The Cosmic Laws that apply here are not known to even your most gifted scientists—even those who call themselves "geniuses".

A Soul who ascends has many choices: they can go to Earth2, they can become [Spirit] Guides and they can ask to travel on Federation ships that are fifth-dimensional. We will also say that many Souls will end up going to new planets in the Golden Universe.

We want to tell you that God's plan has been changed several times. He originally had the Earth Changes happening much sooner. The additional time was given so more could Awaken and indeed, they have. He also has carefully planned many other events to help even more Awaken.

Archangel Gabriel ⌒ The 'Norway Spiral' was our [the Angelic Kindom's] way of waking up mankind.

Ascended Masters ⌒ We believe [the authors] will be able to help people [Awaken] through this book also. Ascension is truly just the beginning. As newly Ascended beings you will be closer to God. You will enjoy a new way of living that is unlike anything you have known before.

We of Telos are giving this information in the hopes that the people who read it will believe and ask for the *Rites of Initiation*. We have heard all the questions of our initiates and tried to answer as many as possible here.

Sheylana ⌒ I will tell you that you are surrounded by help on all sides. Never are you alone. We of Telos are here to guide you, love you and teach you if you only let us. ✴

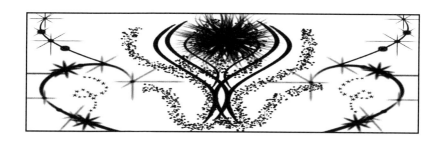

RESOURCES AND REFERENCES

Books

ANNA, GRANDMOTHER OF JESUS: A MESSAGE OF WISDOM AND LOVE, Claire Heartsong. ISBN: 978-0937147346.

MANTRA MEDITATION: CHANGE YOUR KARMA WITH THE POWER OF SACRED SOUND, Thomas Ashley-Farrand. ISBN: 978-1591791774.

TELOS V1: REVELATIONS OF A NEW LEMURIA, Aurelia L. Jones. ISBN: 978-0970090249.

TELOS V2: MESSAGES FOR THE ENLIGHTENMENT OF A HUMANITY IN TRANSFORMATION, Aurelia L. Jones. ISBN: 978-0970090256.

TELOS V3: PROTOCOLS OF THE FIFTH DIMENSION, Aurelia L. Jones. ISBN: 978-0970090270.

THE ASCENSION FLAME OF PURIFICATION AND IMMORTAL-ITY, Aurelia L. Jones. ISBN: 978-0970090294.

THE OTHER KINGDOMS SPEAK OUT, Gail Ries. ISBN: 978-0977710614.

THE PLEIADAN AGENDA, Barbara Hand Clow. ISBN: 978-1879181304.

THE RINGING CEDAR SERIES: THE NEW CIVILIZATION (Book 8.1), Vladimir Megré. ISBN: 978-980181272.

THE RINGING CEDAR SERIES: WHO ARE WE? (Book 5), Vladimir Megré. ISBN: 978-980181241.

THE VORTEX: WHERE THE LAW OF ATTRACTION ASSEMBLES ALL COOPERATIVE RELATIONSHIPS, Esther and Jerry Hicks. ISBN: 978-1401918828.

TREE TALK, Dianne Robbins. ISBN: 978-1425185411.

CDs

EARTH 2 AND YOU (CD), Karen Cook, Benu Too Inc., Albuquerque, NM.

Endnotes

1. Ries, Gail and Marc. *2012 - Mother Earth Wants You!* TBD.
2. Cook, Karen. *Lyra, Lemuria and Mu: Lost and Found (CASSETTE).* Benu Too Inc., Albuquerque, NM.
3. Ries, Marc and Gail. *(Global) First Contact Protocols and Warnings*. (The Other Kingdoms Speak Out: November 1, 2009). Retrieved January 8, 2010 from http://theotherkingdoms.com/website/speak_out.html.
4. Ibid. *2012 - Mother Earth Wants You!*
5. Ibid.
6. Cook, Karen. *Water Blessing from "Lyra, Lemuria and Mu: Lost and Found" Benu Workshop June, 2005 (HANDOUT).* Benu Too Inc., Albuquerque, NM.
7. Ibid. *2012 - Mother Earth Wants You!*

8. Cook, Karen. *The Silence of Spiritual Growth (CD)*. Benu Too Inc., Albuquerque, NM: May 2, 2009).

9. Ries, Gail. *The Other Kingdoms Speak Out.* OR: The Other Kingdoms, 2009.

10. Ibid. *2012 - Mother Earth Wants You!*

11. Ibid.

12. Schucman, Helen. *A Course in Miracles*. CA: Foundation for Inner Peace, 2007.

INDEX

L

Law of Attraction 115
Laws of Science 99
Lemuria xvii, 28, 30, 31, 34, 44
Lemurian 26, 30, 31, 44
Lemurian Crystal 26, 31, 33
Lemurians 26, 28
Life Review 79
Lightworkers 22, 56, 60
Little Mu 30. *See* Lemuria
Living Library 30, 33
Lizard People 29, 30, 31, 48
Lord Sananda xvi
Lord Serapis Bey 81
Lost Souls of Mu 28, 41
Luxor 80
Lyra 26

M

male and female energies xix
mantra vii, xv
Mass Ascension 68, 89
meditation 62
merkabas 93
Mother Earth 42, 116
Mount Shasta xiii, xix, 34
Mu 27, 29, 30, 41

N

Namaste
    definition of xix
    Reiki symbol 39, 49, 65
negativity 60, 61

O

of the Dark
    3D races in the Universe 92
    as not being evil 61
    definition of xix
    keeping information from those xi
    those of the higher dimensions 61

The Other Kingdoms Speak Out
Gail Ries
ISBN: 978-0977710614

Through their words, they tell not only stories about their lives but also messages of love, hope and concern for our future. With humor, courage and grace the shining examples of their integrity, love and friendship towards man comes through. We are allowed glimpses into not only their Kingdoms but we see our world in a whole new light.

"[The Other Kingdoms Speak Out] is so beautiful and every passage I read clears away the veil bit by bit. I feel transported to the elemental kingdom through just reading a few words..."
—**Susan, MT**.

"I think it is great. I have read through it and find it delightful. The personal comments from the other kingdoms are a consciousness shift. It is wonderful to know how these beings think and feel."
—**Valerie, CA**.

Visit TheOtherKingdoms.com for more info.

2012 - Mother Earth Wants You!
Gail & Marc Ries

Mother Earth is a wonderful being. Her soul is very old, but her heart is young. Even though humanity treats her with disrespect, she loves and cares for us all. She wants very much to ascend and wants to take as many of you with her as possible. It is our hope that humanity will Awaken and take up the goal of healing Mother Earth and helping her to ascend.

"We have watched your progress from caveman to a modern society. You have endured Duality for millions of years and now—in a spectacular event—it is time for the experiment to be over. If you are ready, you can join us in the stars."
—Serpina the Centarian

"Your government does not want you remembering your Divinity because they cannot enslave you if you know about Light and Love."
-Anadarian the Arcturian

"I am a Pleiadian from your future. I wish to add to your knowledge about the government's treachery. They have kept many secrets from your people, including those that I will now tell you."
—Janadoria the Pleiadian